Praise

Standing for God in America

If you are a seasoned follower of Jesus Christ, or a new believer, this book is an enlightening reminder that as Christians we are all called to make a difference. Lynn uses the power and truth of God's Word to guide us to a better understanding so that we will be equipped and motivated to make a stand for God in our families and communities. Through her writing it is evident that Lynn loves to spend time with the Lord and studying his word.

—Darcy Turner Med, Elementary Principal, Faith Christian School Summerville, SC

***

Many Americans believe that our country is in the midst of a moral crisis! It is not only obvious to Christians, but to people of other faith groups, as well. There is no question in the mind of many Americans that our nation is headed in the wrong direction, morally, spiritually, and socially. But the question is: Can we do anything about it? Is there hope that we return to the fundamental Judeo Christian principles on which our nation was founded?

This book offers us hope. It is an encouraging read, but a challenging one, as well. It will take the same kind of effort that built our nation to restore our nation. I recommend this book for anyone who wants to see things change for the better and are willing to work to make it happen.

—Stan Cruse, Pastor, Fellowship of Oakbrook, Retired Army Chaplain (Maj)

***

Lynn's book is a comprehensive coverage of the major challenges we face as Christians in our modern world and provides the Biblical foundation we need to apply our faith to each challenge. This thought-provoking book is invaluable for all Christ-followers and all who are interested in living aligned with God's Word.

—**Mark Wise, Esq.,** *Charlotte O. Wise,* CAPT, JAGC, USN, Retired

STANDING FOR GOD IN AMERICA

*How Christians Can
Make a Difference in
Today's Society*

Lynn S. Wogamon

Scriptural Reference

To Chris, the love of my life.

You have been my rock for over 40 years
and have given me the courage to try new things.

Thank you for your love and faith in me!

Table of Contents

Preface

I love God, I love America, and I love people! There is no doubt that our country is facing multiple challenges, including unemployment, racial unrest, immigration challenges, and political division. One evening as I was watching the news, I told my husband that most of the challenges we face as a country could be easily resolved if God's Word was applied to each situation. I also noted that most people do not know Scripture and the truth it contains. He looked me in the eye and said, "Tell them!" I have continued to feel the Holy Spirit's leading to share God's wisdom and plan with others. *Standing for God in America: How Christians Can Make a Difference in Today's Society* presents biblical answers to the issues affecting America today. It also highlights ways Christians can become involved in their communities and across the nation to make an impact for God.

I believe that many Christians are frustrated, confused, and even angry at what is happening in the United States. They want to see change, but don't know what to do or how to get involved. My prayer is that this book will give readers knowledge of what God's Word says about important topics, guidance to know what to do, and encouragement to begin "standing for God."

Standing is easy when there are no winds and the weather is calm. It is much more difficult to stand firm when winds are blowing, waves are crashing, and a storm is in full force against you, but God's Word says those who persevere will lack nothing.

"Consider it pure joy, my brothers and sisters, whenever you face trials of many kinds, because you know that the testing of your faith produces perseverance. Let perseverance finish its work so that you may be mature and complete, not lacking anything." (James 1:2-4)

May we who are called to be "Christ-followers" share Him with the world, starting here in America.

"Three Things"

I know three things must always be

To keep a nation strong and free.

One is a hearthstone bright and dear,

With busy, happy loved ones near.

One is a ready heart and hand

To love and serve and keep the land.

One is a worn and beaten way

To where the people go to pray.

So long as these are kept alive,

Nation and people will survive.

God keep them always everywhere-

The home, the heart, the place of prayer.

Author unknown
in *The Moral Compass,* William J. Bennett

Part 1 Introduction

CURRENT STATE OF AMERICA

The United States is the greatest country in the world! I say this not because I live here and not because I look at everything through rose-colored glasses. I can, without reservation, state that America is great because it was founded on Judeo-Christian beliefs and has remained strong in these beliefs for almost 250 years. It is still a country where a person is free to pursue his interests and, regardless of background, achieve his dreams. It is a country where people can unite as Americans while holding onto their cultural heritage. It is a country of dreamers and innovators who are always striving to improve our world. It is a country of givers, people who are willing to help others - whether next door or far away.

Unfortunately, this America I know and love is in crisis. We are facing social, political, and foreign challenges, as well as economic difficulties that may impact our citizens for generations. Over the past few decades, we have seen a decline in morality and traditional family values; our Judeo-Christian beliefs have come under attack. I believe that at the core of these issues is a growing apathy towards God's Word. Many people are asking, "Where is the America I once knew?" At the risk of painting too bleak a picture, it is important to recognize where we are as a country so we may look for solutions to the growing challenges we face.

Social Issues

Social issues have become the focus of national attention. Racial inequality and unrest are topics of concern. Recent incidents involving African-Americans and law enforcement have ignited racial conflicts –

some quite violent - in cities and communities across the nation. Hate crimes against all races have increased, including attacks on Asian and Jewish individuals. Critical race theory (CRT), as it relates to our institutions, businesses, education system, and social structure, is now a major topic of discussions and debate. CRT has been described as an intellectual and social movement centered on the premise that race is not a natural, biologically grounded feature of distinct subgroups of humans, but rather was culturally invented in order to oppress and exploit people of color.[1] Critical race theorists seek to apply this concept for the goal of eliminating all race-based or other unjust social structures. This theory has been adopted as part of the curriculum and mission in many businesses and school districts.[2]

Ecological concerns related to climate change and sustainability are entering into the political and legal arenas. According to CNN, "...climate change weaves through our daily lives -- from global politics and business to sea levels and weather to the clothes we wear and the food we eat."[3] Governmental regulations on business and industry include limiting the use of fossil fuels, decreasing greenhouse gas emissions, and reducing "carbon footprints." Executive orders and legislation limiting oil production have led to an interest in alternative sources of power. Solar panels, and wind turbines are available for home use, and electric vehicles are becoming popular.

America has also witnessed a rise in violence over the past few years. Major cities have seen increases in the number of gun-related and aggravated assaults, while law enforcement has come under attack. "Smash and grab" thefts occur with no attempt to stop the crime; repeat offenders are often released on bail. Unfortunately, the growing distrust and lack of respect for law enforcement, not to mention cuts in funding, have led to a shortage of police officers. Fewer officers on duty means less safety for citizens.

Finally, the trade in illicit drugs and human trafficking have become areas of concern across the country. Fentanyl, a synthetic opioid that is 50-100 times more potent than morphine, is often added to illegal drugs such as heroin and cocaine.[4] As a result, deaths from drug overdoses have dramatically increased in recent years. Human trafficking, including sex trafficking involving women and children, is on the rise in every state. Additionally, it's believed that 12.3 million people are forced into labor and 2.4 million of those are the result of labor trafficking.[5]

Political and Economic Issues

The 2020 national elections highlighted the fact that the political divide in this country was greater than ever. Election results suggest that there are significant differences among our citizens with respect to the function of government and the direction of our country. There are growing concerns regarding the integrity of the election process, the most fundamental component of our democracy.

America also faces foreign challenges as tensions escalate and countries across the globe go to war. Our leaders face serious decisions regarding America's role in these conflicts. At home, immigration remains a source of concern. Thousands of illegal immigrants, or refugees, enter this country through our southern border, creating a humanitarian and security crisis.

Financially, America is in a period of inflation. Fuel and food prices have soared, while shortages of many core materials have limited production of goods. Interruptions in the supply chain cause delays in fulfilling customer orders, leading to unprecedented shortages of daily items. Interest rates are on the rise, and on top of everything else, the national debt has reached $30 trillion, suggesting long-term financial uncertainty for Americans.[6]

Family and Religious Issues

Closer to home, the attack on the concept of the nuclear family is raging. According to World Population Review, approximately 50% of married couples in the United States divorce, the sixth-highest divorce rate in the world.[7] Subsequent marriages have an even higher divorce rate. Same-sex marriages are becoming more common, and nearly 200,000 children live with same-sex parents.[8] Abortion laws are a hot topic right now. In June 2022, the Supreme Court overturned the 1973 Roe v. Wade decision that legalized abortion, finding it was unconstitutional. The Court ruled that laws regarding abortion should be made at the state level.[9] Additionally, gender and LGBTQ rights advocates remain in the spotlight, calling for acceptance and normalization of these non-traditional lifestyle and perspective choices. These issues lead to a growing concern about the future of the traditional family.

Finally, churches and Christian leaders face opposition as they work to witness and minister within their communities, with many godly men and women now confronting a new form of opposition known as "cancel culture." Merriam-Webster defines this new phenomenon as "the practice or tendency of engaging in mass canceling as a way of expressing disapproval and exerting social pressure."[10] This movement aims to censor books, social media, and even public appearances by anyone presenting a Christian world-view. Additionally, churches across the country have dealt with forced shut-downs and exclusion from being able to rent public facilities for worship. Christian foster care and adoption services have lost their licensure for their refusal to place children with unmarried or same-sex couples. [11]

Faced with the enormity of our current, critical situation, it would be easy to despair about America's future. But there is hope. Grassroot movements are underway all across our country to address the multitude of concerns we face. A growing number of Christians have become committed to involvement at local, state, and national levels. These men and women demonstrate a willingness to take a stand for godly values and principles. They are actively looking for ways they can make a difference in the midst of these trying times. Join me as we learn how we can Stand for God in America!

AMERICA'S GODLY HISTORY

God has been an integral part of America's history since its beginning. Over four hundred years ago, people from other parts of the world set out for a "new world" that they prayed would offer a better life. They left family and friends to face danger and adversity, seeking wealth, freedom from slavery, and freedom to worship God without interference.[1] In 1607, the Virginia Company of England established the first permanent British colony in Jamestown. Tobacco proved successful and quickly became a profitable export. Many came to America to escape from slavery. Half of the settlers in the southern colonies arrived as indentured servants, agreeing to work from four to seven years to pay for their passage. Once this service was completed, they were given a small tract of land in the colony.

Others came to America for religious freedom. Lord Baltimore of England founded the colony of Maryland. William Penn, a wealthy Quaker and friend of King Charles II, was given a large tract of land west of the Delaware River. Penn encouraged others from Europe to come by promising them religious freedom. Many groups, including Quakers, Amish, Baptists, and Mennonites, settled in this area. Some seeking religious freedom settled in the New England area. These "Pilgrims" had previously left England to go to Holland, but when given the opportunity to establish a new settlement, they chose to come to America. In 1630, a group of 900 Puritans led by John Winthrop emigrated to the new land. Each of these groups brought with them a religious fervor and desire to worship God in their own way.

The Faith of our Founding Fathers

Over the next 150 years, more people came to the colonies to establish businesses and create a new life for their families. England, however, continued to view the colonists as British citizens, demanding they pay taxes. As the colonists became more frustrated with these high taxes, discussions about rebellion against England began spreading among the people. Emotions reached a boiling point with the institution of the Coercive Acts against Boston in 1774, prompting leaders throughout the colonies to meet in Philadelphia. The Coercive Acts were imposed by the British Parliament as punishment for the Boston Tea Party.[2] In response, the first Continental Congress, held in Carpenter's Hall, met to define American rights and organize a plan of resistance. George Washington, John Adams, and John Jay were among the delegates for this first meeting. Over the coming years, this group of men led in drafting the Declaration of Independence, the Articles of Confederation, and the US Constitution. The following men are generally considered our country's Founding Fathers:

John Adams	Patrick Henry	George Mason
Samuel Adams	John Jay	James Monroe
John Dickenson	Thomas Jefferson	Thomas Paine
Benjamin Franklin	Richard Henry Lee	Benjamin Rush
Alexander Hamilton	James Madison	Roger Sherman
John Hancock	John Marshall	George Washington

These early leaders were men of faith. They were willing to risk their lives and the lives of their families in pursuit of freedom. In recent years, there has been much debate over the depth of the founding fathers' faith, however, it is evident from their writings and speeches that they recognized God as their spiritual leader and actively sought His wisdom in all actions and decisions. Nearly every one of the fifty-five men who wrote the Constitution were members of orthodox Christian churches and many were outspoken evangelicals. In addition, more than half of these men received degrees from schools that today would be considered seminaries.[3] Here are just a few examples of their writings, demonstrating the faith of these remarkable leaders.

George Washington is often referred to as the First Founding Father. Throughout his military and political careers, he frequently named God as the source of his strength and wisdom. Perhaps one of the best ways to get insight into Washington's spiritual life is through his daily prayers. His personal prayer book was discovered in 1891, containing twenty-four pages of morning and evening prayers.[4] Consider the following prayer for Sunday morning:

> Almighty God, and most merciful Father, who didst command the children of Israel to offer a daily sacrifice to Thee, that thereby they might glorify and praise Thee for Thy protection both night and day; receive, O Lord, my morning sacrifice, which I now offer up to Thee...I beseech Thee, my sins, remove them from Thy presence, as far as the east is from the west, and accept of me for the merits of Thy Son, Jesus Christ, that when I come into Thy temple, and compass Thine altar, my prayers may come before Thee as incense; and as Thou wouldst hear me calling upon Thee in my prayers, so give me grace to hear Thee calling on me in Thy word, that it may be wisdom, righteousness, reconciliations and peace to the saving of my soul in the day of the Lord Jesus.

For generations, Washington's Farewell Address was required learning in public schools. In his final speech before retiring from public service, Washington stated, "Of all the dispositions and habits which lead to political prosperity, religion and morality are indispensable supports. In vain would that man claim the tribute of patriotism, who should labor to subvert these great pillars."[5]

John Quincy Adams, our nation's second president, agreed with Washington. He stated, "The general principles on which the fathers achieved independence were…the general principles of Christianity."[6] Later, on July 4, 1837, an elderly John Adams gave a patriotic speech in Massachusetts. He began his address saying,

> Why is it that, next to the birthday of the Savior of the World, your most joyous and most venerated festival returns on this day (i.e., on the Fourth of July)? Is it not that in the chain of human events, the birthday of the nation is indissolubly linked with the birthday of the Savior? That it forms a leading event in the progress of the gospel dispensation? Is it not that the Declaration of Independence first organized the social compact on the foundation of the Redeemer's mission upon earth? That it laid the cornerstone of human government upon the first precepts of Christianity?

Recent historians often refer to Benjamin Franklin and Thomas Jefferson as the two least religious Founding Fathers but when compared with most people today, they would be considered quite religious. For example, Franklin drafted a statewide prayer proclamation in his home state of Pennsylvania and recommended Christianity in the state's public schools.[7] Jefferson, concerned that the United States might disregard God's laws of right and wrong, wrote,

> God who gave us life gave us liberty. Can the liberties of a nation be secure when we have removed a conviction that these liberties are the gift of God? Indeed I tremble for my country when I reflect that God is just, that His justice cannot sleep forever. Commerce between master and slave is despotism. Nothing is more certainly written in the book of fate than that these people are to be free.[8]

Let's close this section with a few quotes from some of the lesser known Founding Fathers:

> Unto Him who is the author and giver of all good, I render sincere and humble thanks for His manifold and unmerited blessings, and especially for our redemption and salvation by His beloved Son...Blessed by His holy name. *John Jay* (Original Chief Justice of the US Supreme Court) [9]

> My only hope of salvation is in the infinite transcendent love of God manifested to the world by the death of His Son upon the Cross. Nothing but His blood will wash away my sins (Acts 22:15). I rely exclusively upon it. Come, Lord Jesus! Come quickly! (Revelation 22:20) *Dr. Benjamin Rush* (founder of The First Day Society and signer of the Constitution)[10]

> I believe that there is one only living and true God, existing in three person, the Father, the Son, and the Holy Ghost...[and] that at the end of this world there will be a resurrection of the dead and a final judgment of all mankind when the righteous what be publicly acquitted by Christ the Judge and admitted to everlasting life and glory, and the wicked be sentenced to everlasting punishment. *Roger Sherman* (signer of both the Declaration and the Constitution)[11]

Faith Permeates the New Nation

Christian faith was evident in many ways in early America. From governmental documents and Supreme Court rulings to churches, and from the education of children to the culture of the day, America's first citizens recognized God as the source of the ideals upon which this country was founded.

Our nation's founding document, the Declaration of Independence, explicitly expresses these Christian ideals. The opening lines read:

> When in the Course of human Events, it becomes necessary for one People to dissolve the Political Bands which have connected them with another, and to assume among the Powers of the Earth, the separate and equal Station to which the Laws of Nature and of Nature's God entitle them, a decent Respect to the Opinions of Mankind requires that they should declare the causes which impel them to the Separation. We hold these Truths to be self-evident, that all Men are created equal, that they are endowed by their Creator with certain unalienable Rights, that among these are Life, Liberty, and the pursuit of Happiness...[12]

The Supreme Court later lent support to the idea of America as founded on Christianity. In 1892, citing more than sixty historical precedents, the Court concluded, "There is no dissonance in these declarations. There is a universal language pervading them all, having one meaning; they affirm and reaffirm that this is a religious nation...this is a Christian nation."[13]

Many of the Founding Fathers were Puritans and held to the Calvinistic theology that man is innately sinful. To ensure that the country's leaders would not become tyrants, the writers of the Constitution proposed three distinct branches of government as described in Isaiah 33:22. The legislative, executive, and judicial branches were to operate independently, thereby serving as a "checks and balances" system for the governing of the nation.[14] Additionally, the idea of "separation of church and state" is not endorsed in either of these documents. So where did the phrase come from? The statement was first made by Jefferson when writing to a group of Baptists in Danbury, Connecticut who were concerned that the government might try to restrict their religious expression. Jefferson wrote that there exists "a wall of separation between church and state" that would prevent governmental interference or restriction.[15] He explained that the intention was that the church would be protected from the state rather than the state being protected from the church.

In the early years of our nation, churches were prominent features in cities, towns, and communities and. served not only as places of worship, but also as schools, centers of mission outreach, and as social gathering places. Ministers were generally respected and held a place of prominence in the community. One well established practice during this time was the preaching of sermons dealing with citizenship and the election process. These Election Sermons, first documented in 1634 in Virginia, were preached throughout the country to remind Christians that they had a dual citizenship, both in heaven and on earth. People were reminded that God had placed them in America with the responsibility to participate in a government that belonged to "We the People."[16]

America's faith could also be seen in its schools and music. In early America, all schools were religious, associated with different groups such as the Quakers and the Puritans. Even early state-funded public schools in Massachusetts had devotional Bible readings and prayers.[17]

The *New England Primer* was used to teach reading to students from 1690 to 1930. In this schoolbook, each letter of the alphabet was accompanied by a Bible verse. Students were expected to learn not only the letter, but also the verse associated with it. For example, the letter B was accompanied by the verse, *"Better is little with the fear of the Lord than great wealth and trouble therewith"* (Proverbs 15:16 [KJV]). National songs such as *The Star-Spangled Banner* and *America, the Beautiful* included references to God and His providence over our country. The final verse of our national anthem is seldom sung today, but its words speak beautifully of the faith of those who founded America:

> O thus be it ever when freemen shall stand
> Between their lov'd home and the war's desolation!
> Blest with vict'ry and peace may the heav'n rescued land
> Praise the power that hath made and preserv'd us a nation!
> Then conquer we must, when our cause it is just,
> And this be our motto – "In God is our trust,"

And the star-spangled banner in triumph shall wave
O'er the land of the free and the home of the brave.[18]

Another well-loved song, *My Country, 'Tis of Thee*, served as our national anthem for nearly one hundred years.[19] Samuel Francis Smith, a young Baptist seminary student, was asked by composer Lowell Mason to translate several German song books. Inspired by one of the songs, *God Bless Our Native Land*, he wrote new lyrics for the tune. Unknown to Smith, this same tune was also used for the British national anthem. Smith's version was first performed by a children's choir in Boston in 1831. It continues to be a favorite among children and adults, alike. The final verse reminds us again of our country's love for God:

Our fathers' God, to Thee,
Author of liberty,
To Thee we sing;
Long may our land be bright,
With freedom's holy light,
Protect us by Thy might,
Great God, our King.

Finally, America's Christian heritage can be found throughout its architecture and monuments. In his article, *God in Our Nation's Capital*, Kerby Anderson highlights a few of these Christian references found in Washington D.C.[21]

The Capitol Building: In the Rotunda, visitors may view paintings of the Pilgrims observing a day of prayer and fasting and of DeSoto placing a crucifix in the ground upon discovering the Mississippi River. At the east entrance to the Senate chamber are engraved the words "Annuit Coeptis" meaning "God has favored our undertakings." Also, in the Capitol's Chapel is a stained glass window depicting George Washington in prayer with the inscription, "In God We Trust."

The Washington Monument: There are numerous carved tribute blocks with quotes such as "Holiness to the Lord," "Search the Scriptures," "The memory of the just is blessed," "May Heaven to this union continue its beneficence," and "Train up a child in the way he should go, and when he is old, he will not depart from it."

The Lincoln Memorial: Inside this memorial, two of Abraham Lincoln's speeches are engraved on the walls. On Lincoln's left side is the Gettysburg Address and on the right is his second inaugural address. In this short speech (703 words), he mentions God fourteen times and quotes two verses.

The Supreme Court Building: There are several places throughout the Supreme Court building with images of Moses with the Ten Commandments. They can be seen over the east portico, inside the courtroom, over the chair of the Chief Justice, and on the bronze doors of the Supreme Court.

As we look back at our country's history, it becomes clear that America was founded on a strong faith in God and a desire to follow His ways. Any attempt to deny this requires ignoring or rewriting much of our past. Instead, we should be grateful to those who came before us. Let us be thankful for our biblical foundation, recognize our purpose to remain a God-fearing nation, and fervently pray that He will bless us and keep us a strong nation under God.

BEING CHRISTIAN IN AMERICA

As we consider the role of Christians in America, we must ask ourselves, "Are we Christians who are also Americans? Or are we Americans who are also Christian?" Is there a difference and does it matter? Before we look at this, we must first consider two concepts that are frequently misused and misunderstood. Patriotism and nationalism are terms people often use interchangeably, suggesting there is no difference between them, but there are distinct differences. Patriotism is about loyalty and pride for one's country. It is a willingness to defend it against aggression and is necessary in order to remain free from rule by another country. We show patriotism when we volunteer for military service, as well as when we honor and support our soldiers and veterans. We demonstrate patriotism when we display the American flag and celebrate Independence Day. Patriotism shines on the faces of athletes as they compete in the Olympics. Patriotism is good and should be encouraged.

Nationalism, however, is about identity and infers that one nation is superior to all others. This type of belief system has led to countless wars and mistreatment of people for centuries. It runs counter to what the Bible teaches. God doesn't put one nation above another. We are all created by Him and He desires that people of every nation know Jesus as Savior. The children's song, *Jesus Loves the Little Children*, reminds us that God loves everyone, regardless of nationality. The song says that "all are precious in his sight." Jesus gave us the Great Commission to preach the gospel throughout the world. When we place America above all other countries, we are not reflecting God's heart.

American Values vs. Christian Values

So is there a difference between what Americans value and what Christians value? Are the two belief systems compatible, or must we choose one over the other? Let's look first at what they have in common. Values such as honesty, fairness, equality, and valuing life are held dear by both believers and non-believers. These values are an inherent part of our laws and moral expectations. The value of caring for those in need is another common value. Secular organizations such as the American Red Cross and the United Way operate alongside religious organizations such as the Salvation Army and the Children's Hunger Fund.

While appreciating the shared values, we must recognize that there are distinctions between American and Christian values. For example, individualism is not a Christian value. While Americans value individual freedoms as an inherent right, Christians recognize that all freedoms, rights and privileges come from being a child of God. We understand that by putting the needs of others above our own as Jesus taught, we often relinquish our own individual freedom for the good of many.

The concept of war is another American value that is not necessarily a Christian value. War in many instances may be the only way for a country to defend itself against invasion. But Jesus also taught that we should *"turn the other cheek"* (Matthew 5:38-40). Christians place value on all life and recognize Jesus' death as the ultimate sacrifice for sin.

Another value that runs counter to Biblical teaching is materialism. In today's American culture, many things compete for our devotion. Excessive attention to material things, pursuit of wealth or power, and excessive devotion to self, job, hobbies, and even family turn our attention from God.[1] It is important for America to be prosperous, as this is a measure of our strength and security on the world stage, but taken to extremes, it becomes a form of idolatry. When we spend more time and energy acquiring possessions than we do investing in the lives of others, we set up these possessions as idols. Instead, we as Christians should measure our strength and security by our degree of faith and reliance on God.

As you can see, differences exist between these two sets of values, but that does not render them mutually exclusive. I believe that as long as we remember that our first priority is to our Lord God, we can embrace many of the common American values. However, we must also realize that our stance on some issues may run counter to popular thought and opinion. The apostle Peter wrote that we are a *"royal priesthood, a holy nation"* (1 Peter 2:9). The King James Version uses the phrase *"peculiar people."* I happen to like the idea of being considered peculiar. Chad Hall writes, "I think it's time for Christians in America (and everywhere) to embrace being weird. Christian values are not American values…We can appreciate and even respect the nation in which we reside, but we must not forget that our status is as foreigner and exiles" (1 Peter 2:11).[2]

Christian Involvement in Government

Based on these differences in values, many ask why Christians should get involved in local and national issues, inferring that we should only spend time and energy on "religious" activities. There are some who believe our first and only priority should be spreading the gospel, and anything that would distract us from our evangelical purpose is in opposition to the mission Christ gave us. Others dismiss involvement in a manner that suggests such involvement in public matters and policy is not appropriate or is unworthy of our attention. David Closson disagrees, saying "…the gospel is a holistic message with implications for all areas of life, including how Christians engage the political process."[3]

Closson suggests a few reasons Christians should be involved in government and the political process. First, the Christian worldview affects all areas of life. He writes:

> Engaging in 'good works' should include participating in the political process because of the legitimate and significant role of government. The decisions made by government have a substantial impact on people and the way we interact with them. A Christian worldview should include a political theology that recognizes every area of life must be included in the 'good works' of believers, especially politics, an area with significant real-life implications for people.

Christians should be involved in public matters because a strong, positive government restrains evil and promotes good. This type of government fosters an environment of peace and welfare for its citizens.

Unfortunately, because government is composed of humans, with their weaknesses, vices, and self-interests, it may also foster unrest and instability. Tyranny, abuse, genocide, and slavery have been supported by various world governments throughout history. When we ignore what is going on around us and allow these evils to continue without acting, we become complicit in the outcomes. It is important that Christians speak out against evil practices and speak up for those who need help. Erwin Lutzer, in his book, *When a Nation Forgets God,* provides a poignant eyewitness account from a Christian in Germany during the Nazi reign. As you read, consider what your response would have been:

> I lived in Germany during the Nazi Holocaust. I considered myself a Christian. We heard stories of what was happening to the Jews, but we tried to distance ourselves from it, because, what could anyone do to stop it?

A railroad track ran behind our small church and each Sunday morning we could hear the whistle in the distance and then the wheels coming over the tracks. We became disturbed when we heard the cries coming from the train as it passed by. We realized that it was carrying Jews like cattle in the cars!

Week after week, the whistle would blow. We dreaded to hear the sound of the wheels because we knew that we would hear the cries of the Jews en route to a death camp. Their screams tormented us. We knew the time the train was coming and when we heard the whistle blow we began singing hymns. By the time the train came past our church we were singing at the top of our voices. If we heard the screams, we sang more loudly and soon we heard them no more.

Years have passed and no one talks about it anymore. But I still hear the train whistle in my sleep. God forgive me; forgive all of us who called ourselves Christians yet did nothing to intervene.[4]

Lutzer further writes, "With every challenge to our liberties, we have another opportunity to prove our love for Christ and the gospel."

History also records many instances where abuses and discrimination were stopped because Christians spoke out. For example, William Wilberforce, a committed Christian, was the driving force behind the successful effort to abolish the slave trade in England.[5] In the United States, Reverend Martin Luther King, Jr. led the civil rights movement to end racism and discrimination.[6]

"Politicians" in the Bible

The Bible provides many examples of people who served as political leaders. First, there were kings who followed God as they ruled. David, Solomon, Josiah, and Nebuchadnezzar are a few of the God-fearing kings who led Israel in worshiping and obeying God. We also find examples of others who, while not kings, served in leadership or government positions. In the Old Testament, Joseph was placed in a public position of leadership by Pharoah. He oversaw the collection and distribution of grain prior to and during the years of famine in Egypt (Genesis 41: 39-49). Moses was given the responsibility of leading (i.e., governing) the nation of Israel. To accomplish this huge task, he assigned men to serve as judges over the tribes (Exodus 18:19-26). These judges handled the daily affairs of each tribe, thus allowing Moses to spend his time seeing to the overall welfare of the nation. In the book of Esther, we read how a young Jewish woman became queen of Persia. When she learned that the Jews were to be killed, Esther risked her life to petition the king on their behalf. Daniel and Nehemiah are two other notable government leaders in the Old Testament. Their stories can be found in the books bearing their names.

In the New Testament, the nation of Israel had come under Roman rule. Without political leadership, Jewish religious leaders, the Pharisee and Sadducees, served as the primary authority in all public matters. During Jesus' travels, He encountered many of these religious leaders, as well as Roman political and military leaders. While most of the religious leaders were opposed to Jesus, there were some who recognized Him as God's Son. He showed kindness and compassion to them, healing a synagogue official's daughter (Mark 5:22-23, 35-43) and a centurion's slave (Luke 7:1-10). He accepted dinner invitations from Pharisees (Luke 11:37) and had conversations about eternal life with a rich young ruler (Luke 18:18-30). Joseph of Arimathea, a prominent member of the Council, spoke on Jesus' behalf several times. He was so devoted to Jesus that following Jesus' death he went to Pilate and requested His body. He personally oversaw Jesus' preparation and burial (John 19:38-42).

The Role of the Church

We have looked at the Christian's role in government and public matters. But what about the church? Should the church as a body of believers get involved as well? Would involvement help or hinder the church's evangelistic mission? Many churches fear that involvement will cause them to lose their tax-exempt status or will alienate current members. First, we should note that pastors can talk about political issues without losing their tax-exempt status. The only stipulation is that no specific candidate or elected official may be promoted or spoken against. In his book, *40 Days Towards a More Godly Nation,* Neil Mammen tells pastors, "You can and should promote propositions that enact biblical principles and encourage your congregation to call their senators. You are free to speak out against moral issues. In fact, I believe God commands us to do so."[7]

Other well-meaning Christians advocate prayer as the primary role of the church regarding societal issues. It is true that Jeremiah 29:7 tells us, *"Also, seek the peace and prosperity of the city to which I have carried you into exile. Pray to the Lord for it, because if it prospers, you too will prosper."*

We are also called to action. Micah 6:8 tells us three things that God requires of his people. The first thing we are to do is to *"act justly."* This action results from prayer. The adage, "Pray like it all depends on God and work like it all depends on you," is certainly appropriate in this situation. It is not an "either/or," but a "both/and" expectation. Titus 1:14 says that Jesus gave His life for us, a people who are eager to do good works. "Fixing governments is not evangelism or discipleship, yet it is a loving action to seek the good of your neighbor, the defenseless, and where you live."[8]

I would like to close this chapter with a sobering thought. In recent years, the Christian church has seen a decline in attendance and commitment, along with a loss of respect in society. Those who actively oppose Christianity speak without fear of censure or ridicule. Meanwhile, those who speak Christian truths are "canceled" and touted as evil or irrelevant. The church finds itself in an uncomfortable position. In an opinion article entitled, *The Church In Exile,* Doyle Sager asks if this position could actually be a gift from God. He writes of the church, "Could this be our opportunity to trust in God rather than in our privileged position?...When social and political support are absent and resources are scarce, an amazing thing happens: They learn to trust God.[9]

Part 1 Chapter 3

DOES GOD HAVE A PLAN FOR AMERICA?

Looking back, it is easy to see that Christianity has played an integral role in America's history, but do we believe that God cares about what is happening right now in our nation? Does He have a plan for America's future? It is imperative that each of us comes to terms with these questions. If we believe that God truly cares about our country, we will be motivated to see His will done by becoming involved in our communities, schools, and government. If we don't believe God has a plan for us, we have no reason to invest our time, energy, and resources to improve the state of our nation. Let's consider these questions more closely.

Does God Care About America?

The entire message of the Bible is one of love. We teach young children that God is love. We read 1 Corinthians 13, known as the "love chapter" at some weddings. And we know that God loves us so much that *"He gave his only Son that whoever believes in him shall not perish, but have eternal life"* (John 3:16). Let's look at a few more verses that describe how much God loves His people.

> *For the eyes of the Lord roam throughout the earth, so that he may strongly support those whose heart is completely his.* (2 Chronicles 16:9 [NASB])

> *For as high as the heavens are above the earth, so great is his love for those who fear him.* (Psalm 103:11)

For I am convinced that neither death nor life, neither angels nor demons, neither the present nor the future, nor any powers, neither height nor depth, nor anything else in all creation, will be able to separate us from the love of God that is in Christ Jesus our Lord. (Romans 8:38-39)

This is love: not that we loved God, but that he loved us and sent his Son as an atoning sacrifice for our sins. (1 John 4:10)

God cares what happens to His people and wants to bless us. Jesus said that He loves us and came to give abundant life (John 10:10). The psalmist wrote, *"Let them give thanks to the Lord for his unfailing love and his wonderful deeds for mankind, for he satisfies the thirsty and fills the hungry with good things"* (Psalm 107:8-9). God cares for us individually and collectively. He cares when we struggle and are oppressed. He cares about our children, families, and businesses. He cares for the poor, the sick, and the weak. He even cares when we disobey by acting immorally and unjustly toward others. Regardless of what we do, God desires the best for us. The question then becomes: "Do we care about God?" Are we willing to learn His ways and follow them, knowing that they are for our good? Are we willing to trust Him?

Before we proceed, we must clarify who "God's people" are. When discussing the United States as a godly nation, many people quote scriptures such as:

If my people, who are called by my name, will humble themselves and pray and seek my face and turn from their wicked ways, then I will hear from heaven, and I will forgive their sin and will heal their land.
(2 Chronicles 7:14)

Blessed is the nation whose God is the Lord, the people he chose for his inheritance. (Psalm 33:12)

You are a chosen people, a holy nation, a people belonging to God."
(1 Peter 2:19)

The nation referred to in these passages was originally the nation of Israel. Later, the term was also used to describe the body of believers known as the church. In the Old Testament, God established His covenant with the nation of Israel, that they would be His chosen people. God said to them, *"I will walk among you and be your God, and you will be my people. I am the Lord your God, who brought you out of Egypt"* (Leviticus 26:12-13). When Jesus came and died on the cross for all men (John 3:16), that covenant relationship extended to all who accept Him as their Savior. They become a part of God's family. Paul wrote to the believers at Galatia, *"For you are all sons of God through faith in Christ Jesus"* (Galatians 3:26 [NASB]).

The Bible does not refer to any nation as a Christian nation. "There is not now, nor has there ever been, a nation on earth that collectively bowed its knee to the Lordship of Jesus Christ."[1] However, there are people who love the Lord in every city, town, and suburb across America. Churches and Christian ministries still seek to serve their communities and share the gospel of Jesus. While the Bible doesn't refer to America, (because America wasn't a country at the time of the writing of scripture), we know that God loves and wants to bless those who love Him and His Son, Jesus. As Christians, we should yearn to see His blessings bestowed not just to us personally, but to our families, friends, and communities. We should be willing to do everything we can to share the gospel so that more people can receive the wonderful blessings God has prepared for His people.

Does God Have a Plan for America?

I believe the answer can be found in Jeremiah 29:11, which says, *"For I know the plans I have for you,' declares the Lord, 'plans to prosper you and not to harm you, plans to give you hope and a future.'"* Are these plans spelled out anywhere in detail or are we supposed to figure them out ourselves? God tells us in Isaiah 55, *"For my thoughts are not your thoughts, neither are your ways my ways"* (vs 8). We are also told that man's plans are futile (Psalm 94:11). Rather than try to make our own way, we are told to seek God first. Then through a relationship with Him, we will come to know His will (Deuteronomy 4:29). Finally, although we don't know God's plans or His timing, we can have confidence as followers of Christ that everything God is doing and will do in the future will work for our good (Romans 8:28).

Now that we are confident that God cares about His people and has a plan for us, how does this apply to our nation? Do we as a country hold a special place in God's heart? Are we blessed above all other nations? Is the phrase "God bless America!" a mandate to God? My answer to these questions would be an emphatic "No!" There is no entitlement to God's blessings. Instead, we must become the people described in 2 Chronicles 7:14, people who will become humble, pray, seek God, and turn from sin. To receive God's blessings, we as a nation must be godly and good. David Palmer writes, "The most important feature of a nation, according to the Bible, is not its power or prestige or prosperity but its goodness. Such goodness will be the result of genuinely building the nation's character upon faith in God."[2] He then shares four principles that describes God's view of a good nation: It will be one that:

- cares for the needy and poor (Deuteronomy 15:11)
- welcomes the stranger (Leviticus 19:34)
- defends and lifts up the powerless (Isaiah 1:17)
- and is a place of justice (Amos 5:24)

Psalm 33 describes how God watches over and blesses those nations who trust in Him. Read this beautiful passage of how He stands ready to care for those who love Him:

But the plans of the Lord stand firm forever,
the purposes of his heart through all generations.
Blessed is the nation whose God is the Lord,
the people he chose for his inheritance.

From heaven the Lord looks down
and sees all mankind;
from his dwelling place he watches
all who live on earth—
He who forms the hearts of all,
who considers everything they do.
No king is saved by the size of his army;
no warrior escapes by his great strength.
A horse is a vain hope for deliverance;
despite all its great strength it cannot save.
But the eyes of the Lord are on those who fear him,
on those whose hope is in his unfailing love,
to deliver them from death
and keep them alive in famine.
We wait in hope for the Lord;
He is our help and our shield.
In him our hearts rejoice,
for we trust in his holy name.
May your unfailing love be with us, Lord,
even as we put our hope in you. (vs 11-22)

It is only through trusting in God that a nation can be strong (Psalm 20:7). In his address to the Constitutional Convention, Franklin said,

We have been assured in the sacred writings that 'unless the Lord build [the house], they labor in vain that build it.' I firmly believe this; and I also believe that without God's concurring aid we shall succeed in this political building no better than the Builders of Babel. We shall be divided by our little partial local interests; our projects will be confounded, and we ourselves shall become a reproach and a bye word down to future age.[3]

In 1795, Massachusetts governor and founding father, Samuel Adams, issued a Proclamation for a Day of Public Fasting, Humiliation and Prayer. In this address to the citizens of his state, he urged everyone to call upon God to bless their state and country. While the language is a little different from what we are accustomed to, listen to the heart of this proclamation:

> The supreme Ruler of the Universe, having been pleased, in the course of His Providence, to establish the Independence of the United States of America, and to cause them to assume their rank, among the nations of the Earth, and bless them with Liberty, Peace and Plenty; we ought to be led by Religious feelings of Gratitude; and to walk before Him, in all Humility, according to His most Holy Law. - But, as the depravity of our Hearts has, in so many instances drawn us aside from the path of duty, so that we have frequently offended our Divine and Merciful Benefactor; it is therefore highly incumbent on us, according to the ancient and laudable practice of our pious Ancestors, to open the year by a public and solemn Fast. - That with true repentance and contrition of Heart, we may unitedly implore the forgiveness of our Sins, through the merits of Jesus Christ, and humbly supplicate our Heavenly Father, to grant us the aids of His Grace, for the amendment of our Hearts and Lives, and vouchsafe His smiles upon our temporal concerns.[4]

So, as God's people, what can and should we do to help return America to a nation that God can bless? First, we must be willing to fall on our knees before God, seek Him, and pray for our country. We must be willing to love Him with all our heart, souls, and strength (Deuteronomy 6:5). Then we must get up and get to work, sharing His message and living out His plan in our homes, neighborhoods, cities, and states. I believe that God will honor and bless our efforts and that we will see mighty things take place when we as Christians are willing to stand for God in America.

On the eve of the 2020 national elections, Franklin Graham posted an article on the magazine site Decisiononline.com, writing:

> America is the greatest nation on earth, and it was founded on Christian principles, but many no longer recognize that foundation. We're the ones who've moved, not God. We've taken Him out of our classrooms and universities. We've turned our backs on Him, and now look what we have—a land filled with violence, hatred, immorality and greed. Far too many of our leaders despise the Name of Jesus and are openly hostile to Christianity…I don't know what the results of the election will be. That's in God's sovereign hand. But I do know we are responsible to pray and ask Him to move in our land once again so that we can say, 'Blessed is the nation whose God is the Lord' (Psalm 33:12).[5]

Part 2 Introduction

Several years ago, I purchased a pair of sunglasses from my neighborhood drug store. They appeared stylish, fit properly, and most of all, were within my budget. I put them on and walked to the car. As I drove home, I noticed that everything looked different; the colors were not quite right. I realized that everything had taken on an orange hue. Now don't get me wrong - I like orange, but when apples look like oranges and springtime leaves appear to be a fall-like russet color, it just doesn't feel right. The color of the lens can affect our perception of the things around us.

The same thing can happen when we look at the world through different "lenses." Individualism, materialism, skepticism, and anger are a few of the lenses people use to see the situations, events, and people around them. Their perceptions are significantly affected, often leading to misperceptions and inaccurate understandings. As we learn how to stand for God in our country, it is important that we view life through His perspective. We must view things through the lens of His Word in order to have a clear and accurate understanding of truth.

The Bible, although written thousands of years ago, is still relevant today. Scripture contains all we need to know in order to live a life of faith. Unfortunately, most Christians have spent little time reading and studying the Bible. Because they don't have a basic knowledge of Scripture, they accept whatever they are told as "truth." Second Timothy 2:15 tells us to *"Study and be eager and do your utmost to present yourself to God approved (tested by trial), a workman who has no cause to be ashamed, correctly analyzing and accurately dividing [rightly handling and skillfully teaching] the Word of Truth"* (AMPC). In the following chapters, we will address several issues facing our country, seeing them as God sees them. This will not be a thorough study of every topic, but rather an overview and starting point for you to delve more deeply into specific issues you may face. So, take off your orange-tinted sunglasses and join me in looking at life through the Son-glasses of truth!

Part 2 Chapter 1

MORALITY IN MODERN CULTURE

We have all heard the saying, "If it feels good, do it!" Using this as a compass for determining what we should and shouldn't do will definitely lead us into trouble. So how can we distinguish between good and bad, right and wrong? Is there an absolute standard? Can what was considered bad yesterday be okay today? And who decides what is right and wrong? Let's look at these ideas from God's perspective.

What is Morality?

The term "morality" is usually defined as principles which guide distinguishing right from wrong. In our progressive culture, most people believe that morality is a personal matter, affecting only themselves.[1] They view Scripture as an arbitrary law made up in former times to keep people from enjoying themselves. Others believe in a relative morality, one that changes from age to age and culture to culture. Society decides what is right and wrong, suggesting that morals are based on the circumstances of the moment. Evolutionists have taught that as humans adapt to their surroundings, changes in behavior must be viewed in the context of surviving in the immediate situation. There is no absolute morality. What is the result of this thinking? A look at our global society reveals violence, sexual immorality, crime, divorce, and misery. When the barriers of moral absolutes are removed, man is given permission to indulge in whatever form of pleasure he desires.[2]

Proverbs 29:18 tells us, *"Where there is no message from God, people don't control themselves. But blessed is the one who obeys wisdom's instruction"* (NIRV).

When we remove God from our lives, we deny ourselves the joy and benefits of having and sharing God's love. Instead, we put our own interests above those of our family.[3] Selfishness keeps us from showing our spouse and children the love they deserve. Greed and ambition cause us to put ourselves first, rather than seeking the good for others. David Kinnaman describes this new moral code of self-fulfillment as one replacing a moral code that "seeks to constrain someone's pursuit of personal fulfillment."[4] This new moral code consists of the following ideas:

- The best way to find yourself is by looking within yourself.
- People should not criticize someone else's life choices.
- To be fulfilled in life, you should pursue the things you desire most.
- The highest goal of life is to enjoy it as much as possible.
- People can believe whatever they want as long as it doesn't affect society.
- Any kind of sexual expression between two consenting adults is acceptable.

Even Christians are accepting this new moral code without really considering how it contradicts their religious beliefs. Kinnaman writes, "Living counter to the new morality is an uphill battle...Nearly everything about the broader culture is expertly marketed to appeal to our comfort, well-being, safety, and satisfaction." In addressing morality, Billy Graham noted, "We have changed our moral code to fit our behavior instead of changing our behavior to harmonize with God's moral code."[5]

One of the most amazing concepts in Scripture is the realization that God gives man free will. He did not make us robots, mindlessly doing everything He tells us. We are not "programmed" for obedience. Instead, He desires that we choose to love and serve Him. By choosing Him and His ways, we demonstrate a desire to have a relationship with Him. God has also given man a conscience.

Everyone, whether believer or unbeliever, has this inner voice that guides them in choosing right and wrong. The effectiveness of that conscience is determined by many factors, including past experiences and individual temperament, as well as the presence or lack of moral training from childhood.

> *So I strive always to keep my conscience clear before God and man.* (Acts 24:16)

> *"To the pure, all things are pure, but to those who are corrupted and do not believe, nothing is pure. In fact, both their minds and consciences are corrupted."* (Titus 1:15)

God's Word tells us that when we accept Jesus as our Savior, we receive the presence and power of the Holy Spirit into our lives. This power is not available to non-believers. Jesus promised His followers, *"If you love me, keep my commands. And I will ask the Father, and he will give you another advocate to help you and be with you forever.... But the Advocate, the Holy Spirit, whom the Father will send in my name, will teach you all things and will remind you of everything I have said to you"* (John 14:15-16, 26). As we seek to learn how God wants us to live, we allow the Holy Spirit to guide us to understand His truth.

God's View of Morality

So how can we know what is right and wrong? For Christians, morality is found in doing what God desires as outlined in Scripture. The Ten Commandments given in Exodus 20 provide the foundation for a God-centered morality. The first four commandments focus on our relationship with God. Exodus 20:5 says that He is a "jealous God," desiring that we worship Him with our whole being. He wants us to avoid anything that would stand in the way of a close relationship with Him. The six remaining commandments guide our conduct towards others. Commandments telling us to honor our parents and to avoid adultery are intended to promote strong, happy families, while those telling us not to lie, steal, covet, or murder form the foundation for a safe and secure society.

No one likes being told that they shouldn't do something, especially if it is something they enjoy or are accustomed to. It's easy to see why those who oppose godly morality view the "thou shalt not" commandments as restrictive and perhaps even vengeful, but we need to see these verses from the perspective of God as our Father. Every parent knows that eventually his child will test the boundaries to see how far he can go. This boundary testing may possibly lead to the child doing something that could hurt him. That's why parents start early, teaching concepts such as safety rules, how to choose friends, and how to act responsibly. For our teenagers, we set boundaries for driving, dating, and curfews. We don't do these things to restrict or punish our teens, but to protect them from the foolishness of youth. While God condemns many actions and attitudes, He does so because He knows they can bring us much harm and heartache. Let's examine a few verses to see what God's Word says about our actions and attitudes.

For it is from within, out of a person's heart, that evil thoughts come—sexual immorality, theft, murder, adultery, greed, malice, deceit, lewdness, envy, slander, arrogance and folly. All these evils come from inside and defile a person. (Mark 7:21-23)

They have become filled with every kind of wickedness, evil, greed and depravity. They are full of envy, murder, strife, deceit and malice. They are gossips, slanderers, God-haters, insolent, arrogant and boastful; they invent ways of doing evil; they disobey their parents; they have no understanding, no fidelity, no love, no mercy. Although they know God's righteous decree that those who do such things deserve death, they not only continue to do these very things but also approve of those who practice them. (Romans 1:29-32)

Do you not know that wrongdoers will not inherit the kingdom of God? Do not be deceived: Neither the sexually immoral nor idolaters nor adulterers nor men who have sex with men nor thieves nor the greedy nor drunkards nor slanderers nor swindlers will inherit the kingdom of God. (1 Corinthians 6:9-11)

The acts of the flesh are obvious: sexual immorality, impurity and debauchery; idolatry and witchcraft; hatred, discord, jealousy, fits of rage, selfish ambition, dissensions, factions and envy; drunkenness, orgies, and the like. I warn you, as I did before, that those who live like this will not inherit the kingdom of God. (Galatian 5:19-21)

But the cowardly, the unbelieving, the vile, the murderers, the sexually immoral, those who practice magic arts, the idolaters and all liars— they will be consigned to the fiery lake of burning sulfur. (Revelation 21:8)

While the list is long, it is important that we fully grasp what it is that displeases God. The actions and attitudes from the previous verses can be better understood by arranging them by type: actions against God; sexuality and conduct; actions towards others; personal attitudes, and divisive attitudes.

Actions against God

idolatry   witchcraft   God-haters

Sexual misconduct

sexual immorality   adultery   homosexuality   impurity

Actions towards others

deceit   slander   theft   disobedience

murder   malice   lack of mercy   dishonesty

Social misconduct

debauchery   lewdness   drunkenness   fits of rage

Divisive attitudes

gossip	discord	dissension	factions

Personal Attitudes

greed	arrogance	selfish ambition	envy
hatred	jealousy	cowardice	boastfulness

Instead of focusing only on what God tells us not to do, we should consider that God knows there are certain things that will hurt our relationship with Him (actions against God), hurt our families (sexual conduct), hurt our relationships with others (actions towards others), or hurt our testimony to others (social misconduct, divisive attitudes). God also desires us to have a heart like His so He warns against attitudes that are counter to those of someone who loves Him (personal attitudes).

Positive Morality

Let's now turn our attention from what God tells us not to do to the positive truth-centered morality that He desires for us. God's morality is centered around what Jesus referred to as the greatest commandments - to love God and to love others (Matthew 22:36-38). God's morality emphasizes worshiping Him and being kind to all people (Mark 12:30,31). We are to demonstrate humility (Philippians 2:3), honesty (Exodus 20:16), and integrity (Proverbs 13:6).

> *Finally, brothers, whatever is true, whatever is honorable, whatever is just, whatever is pure, whatever is lovely, whatever is commendable, if there is any excellence, if there is anything worthy of praise, think about these things.* (Philippians 4:8 [ESV])

> *Do your best to present yourself to God as one approved, a worker who does not need to be ashamed and who correctly handles the word of truth.* (2 Timothy 2:15)

In everything, set them an example by doing what is good. In your teaching, show integrity, seriousness and soundness of speech that cannot be condemned, so that those who oppose you may be ashamed because they have nothing bad to say about us. (Titus 2:7-8)

Dear friends, I urge you as foreigners and exiles to abstain from the passions of the flesh, which wage war against your soul. (1 Peter 2:11)

For this very reason, make every effort to add to your faith goodness; and to goodness, knowledge; and to knowledge, self-control; and to self-control, perseverance; and to perseverance, godliness; and to godliness, mutual affection; and to mutual affection, love. For if you possess these qualities in increasing measure, they will keep you from being ineffective and unproductive in your knowledge of our Lord Jesus Christ. (2 Peter 1:5-8)

For every action that God condemns, there is a positive action that He approves and will bless. For example, when we avoid sexual immorality and remain pure and faithful to our spouse, we are blessed with a happy marriage. When we replace dishonesty and gossip with honesty and discretion, we become people others can trust. And when we replace idolatry and witchcraft with a devotion to God, we receive the blessings that come with a personal relationship with the Almighty God.

Let's look back now at the "new moral code" that was previously described. Kinnaman proposes an alternative code that places Jesus at the center. He suggests:

- To find yourself, discover the truth outside yourself, in Jesus.
- Loving others does not always mean staying silent.
- Joy is found not in pursuing our own desires but in giving of ourselves to bless others.
- The highest goal of life is giving glory to God.
- God gives people the freedom to believe whatever they want, but those beliefs always affect society.

God's moral code is not punishment, but rather a blessing from Him. Billy Graham wrote, "The fact that immorality is rampant throughout the nation doesn't make it right. The Ten Commandments are just as valid today as they were when God gave them. They provide the foundation of right living in the sight of God and with others."[6] The apostle Paul wrote that God's grace *"teaches us to say 'No' to ungodliness and worldly passions, and to live self-controlled, upright and godly lives in this present age"* (Titus 2:12). Following His moral code brings joy to everything we do and every relationship we have. May we say with the psalmist, *"I desire to do your will, my God; Your law is within my heart"* (Psalm 40:8).

LEADERSHIP

The picture shows a group of people all headed in the same direction. Behind them, a man is running to catch up, shouting, "Wait for me! I'm your leader!" Hundreds of books and articles have been written on leadership. People attend seminars to acquire people skills, public speaking skills, and salesmanship skills in an effort to learn how to be a leader. The question is, "Do we need more leaders or do we need more *effective* leaders?" Tony Robbins defines leadership as the ability "to influence, inspire and help others become their best selves, building their skills and achieving goals along the way… the ability to inspire a team to achieve a certain goal."[1] As we look at what the Bible says about leadership, we must remember that all leadership authority comes from God.

Romans 13:1-2 tells us, *"Everyone must submit to the governing authorities, for there is no authority except from God, and those that exist are instituted by God"* (HCSB). He is the source of wisdom and discernment necessary to lead successfully. James 1:5 speaks to all who would choose to seek a position of leadership, *"If any of you lacks wisdom, you should ask God, who gives generously to all without finding fault, and it will be given to you."* However, this wisdom is only available to those who believe in Jesus and place their faith in Him (James 1:6). We can be sure that there will be many people in leadership positions who do not know the Lord as their Savior. That doesn't mean that God can't use them. Even non-believers can be strong leaders. The traits of effective leadership apply to everyone, but especially to those who call themselves followers of Christ.

Characteristics of a Godly Leader

Effective leaders possess certain character traits that instill confidence and loyalty in the people they lead. In addition to knowledge and the ability to relate with others, there are qualities that set godly leaders apart from the rest. Let's look specifically at five characteristics that can elevate everyday individuals into effective, godly leaders.

Integrity: Godly leadership must begin with integrity. Someone described integrity as "doing the right thing even when no one is looking." As we look at what the Bible says about leadership, we find verses describing the role of the king. In this context, the title "king" can refer to a political, religious, or military leader. Two of Israel's most successful kings, David and his son, Solomon, wrote extensively about godly leadership. Let's look at a few verses – David in Psalms and Solomon in Proverbs – that focus specifically on integrity:

> *May integrity and uprightness protect me, because my hope, Lord, is in you.* (Psalm 25:21)

> *Because of my integrity you uphold me and set me in your presence forever.* (Psalm 41:12)

> *Whoever walks in integrity walks securely, but whoever takes crooked paths will be found out.* (Proverbs 10:9)

> *The integrity of the upright guides them, but the unfaithful are destroyed by their duplicity.* (Proverbs 11:3)

The leader who demonstrates integrity will say what he means and will do what he says. He will not change his actions and ideas based on who he is with but will be consistent in all matters. The adage, "Practice what you preach," applies here. Jesus called out the religious leaders for being hypocrites, saying, *"So you must be careful to do everything they tell you. But do not do what they do, for they do not practice what they preach. They tie up heavy, cumbersome loads and put them on other people's shoulders, but they themselves are not willing to lift a finger to move them. Everything they do is done for people to see"* (Matthew 23:3-5).

Justice: Another concept closely related to integrity is justice. In the Bible, the king had ultimate power to dole out justice or injustice as he saw fit. If the king had integrity, then he would judge fairly. Solomon describes this justice, saying, *"A king who sits on the throne of justice disperses all evil with his eyes"* (Proverbs 20:8 [NASB1995]) and *"The king gives stability to the land by justice, but a man who takes bribes overthrows it"* (Proverbs 29:4 [NASB1995]). Effective leadership can be described as a cycle of actions: the leader shows integrity (what he does/ how he lives), he demonstrates credibility (by doing what he said he would do), the people trust the leader, and then the people follow. Rick Warren describes it this way: "If you have no credibility, you have no trust. If you have no trust, you have no leadership. Where do leaders get that trust? All trust comes from integrity."[2] Do you see the progression? It must start with the person in leadership living his or her life to a higher standard- a standard of integrity.

Honesty: A close relative of integrity is honesty. Godly leaders are expected to be honest in their words, actions, and intentions. Proverbs 20:28 (NASB) says, *"Loyalty and truth watch over the king, and he upholds his throne by loyalty."* And in chapter 29, we read, *"If a king judges the poor with truth, his throne will be established forever"* (vs 14). There is no such thing as a white lie or little fib in God's sight. Solomon put it more bluntly, saying, *"The Lord detests lying lips, but he delights in people who are trustworthy"* (Proverbs 12:22). Psalm 15 beautifully describes this type of person. Listen to David's words:

> *Lord, who may dwell in your sacred tent?*
>
> *Who may live on your holy mountain?*
>
> *The one whose walk is blameless, who does what is righteous,*
>
> *who speaks the truth from their heart; whose tongue utters no slander,*

who does no wrong to a neighbor, and casts no slur on others; who despises a vile person but honors those who fear the Lord; who keeps an oath even when it hurts, and does not change their mind; who lends money to the poor without interest; who does not accept a bribe against the innocent.

Whoever does these things will never be shaken.

<u>Humility:</u> The third character trait of a godly leader is humility. Jesus changed the entire concept of leadership by saying,

You know that the rulers of the Gentiles lord it over them, and their high officials exercise authority over them. Not so with you. Instead, whoever wants to become great among you must be your servant, and whoever wants to be first must be your slave— just as the Son of Man did not come to be served, but to serve, and to give his life as a ransom for many" (Matthew 20:25-28).

Jesus then gave His followers a vivid picture of humility. On His last night with the disciples, He took off his outer garment, knelt, and washed their dirty feet (John 13:3-17). A few days later, Jesus demonstrated the ultimate humility by submitting to death on the cross. We also read in Scripture that *"God opposes the proud but shows favor to the humble"* (James 4:6). Rick Warren writes, "The Bible tells us that God opposes the proud. That means every time a leader thinks he's 'hot stuff,' God opposes him…And when God opposes a leader, he'll lose the battle. Every time. The Bible says be humble or you'll stumble."[3]

<u>Generosity:</u> Godly leaders are also to demonstrate generosity in their personal and public lives. We will discuss this trait more in the next chapter, but let's note for now that God blesses leaders who are generous. Psalm 112:9 says, *"They share freely and give generously to those in need. Their good deeds will be remembered forever. They will have influence and honor."* Those in leadership and those who have been blessed materially

should also be reminded that *"from everyone who has been given much, much will be demanded; and from the one who has been entrusted with much, much more will be asked"* (Luke 12:48). Leaders often find themselves in situations where the needs of people are evident. A godly leader will use these opportunities to demonstrate a spirit of generosity with his money, time, and resources.

<u>Wisdom:</u> As Christians, we should seek God's wisdom daily. For those in positions of leadership, having God's wisdom and understanding is critical. King Solomon was one of the wisest leaders in the Bible. As he began his reign, he asked God for one thing: *"Give me wisdom and knowledge, that I may lead this people, for who is able to govern this great people of yours?"* (2 Chronicles 1:10). Scripture goes on to say that God was so pleased with this request, He blessed Solomon not only with wisdom, but with riches and peace. Here are a few more verses about wisdom:

> *The mouth of the righteous utters wisdom, and his tongue speaks justice.* (Psalm 37:30)

> *How much better to get wisdom than gold, to get insight rather than silver!* (Proverbs 16:16)

> *Who is like the wise? Who knows the explanation of things? A person's wisdom brightens their face and changes its hard appearance.* (Ecclesiastes 8:1)

Leaders in the Bible

Often, a picture is worth a thousand words. This is especially true as we seek to understand what godly leadership looks like in action. The Bible provides numerous examples of men and women who were placed in positions of leadership and fulfilled their responsibilities with the characteristics previously discussed. Let's take a quick look at just a few of these individuals to see how they lived out their purpose for God.

Old Testament leaders

The Old Testament is filled with stories of great leaders such as Moses, Joshua, David, and Nehemiah. Each of these men was called by God for a specific purpose and actively sought God's guidance, wisdom, and protection. As a result, He blessed them as they led. None was perfect, but each had a love for God, a purpose from God, and obedience to His plan and instructions.

Moses grew up in the home of the Egyptian Pharaoh. After leaving Egypt, God called to Moses through a burning bush to return to lead the Israelites out of Egypt into a land He had promised them (Exodus 3). Moses' initial response to the Lord was one of self-doubt and excuses, but once he realized that God would be with him, he obeyed. The Israelites were not an easy group of people to lead. They faced many challenges on their journey and often complained and criticized Moses' leadership, but Moses remained obedient to what God told him to do. In Exodus 33, we find Moses' prayer for guidance, along with God's response. *"If you are pleased with me, teach me your ways so I may know you and continue to find favor with you. Remember that this nation is your people."* *The Lord replied, "My Presence will go with you, and I will give you rest"* (vs 13-14). This passage also says that the Lord spoke to Moses face to face, just as a man speaks to his friend (vs 11).

Another great leader from the Old Testament is Joshua. As the Israelites approached the Promised Land, they sent a group of men into the area to spy out the land and its people. They saw abundant fruits and vegetation, but also reported that the people of the land were large and powerful. The Israelites became afraid and wanted to appoint another leader to take them back to Egypt. Joshua, one of those who had investigated the new territory, tore his clothes in sadness and called out to his fellow countrymen. He pleaded with them, saying,

The land we passed through and explored is exceedingly good. If the Lord is pleased with us, he will lead us into that land, a land flowing with milk and honey, and will give it to us. Only do not rebel against the Lord. And do not be afraid of the people of the land, because we will devour them. Their protection is gone, but the Lord is with us. Do not be afraid of them." (Numbers 14:7-9).

Shortly before his death, Moses named Joshua as the next leader of the Israelites. Soon afterward, God spoke to Joshua, telling him that Moses had died and he was now to lead the people (Joshua 1:2). He obeyed, following God's guidance and direction in many military battles, including capturing the city of Jericho. As the Israelites entered the land promised to them by God, Joshua called the people to put away all of their idols and worship God. He then challenged them to holiness, saying, *"...but if serving the Lord seems undesirable to you, then choose for yourselves this day whom you will serve... But as for me and my household, we will serve the Lord"* (Joshua 24:15).

David is known as Israel's greatest king but he did not start out as a king or even in the family of the king. As a child, he was a shepherd watching over his father's sheep. Later, as a young teenager, he responded to a challenge issued by Goliath who opposed the Israelites. The story of David killing Goliath with a slingshot and stone is well-known. We see David as a mighty warrior as an adult, but when we read the full account of David's life, we find that his relationship with God was central to his success.

Throughout the Psalms, David expressed his love for God. In Psalm 18, he wrote, *"I love You, O Lord, my strength. The Lord is my rock, my fortress and my deliverer"* (vs 1-2). Later, he wrote, *"One thing I ask from the Lord, this only do I seek: that I may dwell in the house of the Lord all the days of my life, to gaze on the beauty of the Lord and to seek him in his temple"* (Psalm 27:4). David was chosen by God and anointed by the prophet Samuel to be Israel's king. Although he wasn't perfect and made many mistakes, he always repented and returned to God. He was known as a man "after God's own heart" (1 Samuel 13:14).

One final Old Testament leader that deserves mentioning is Nehemiah. He was one of the Israelites who were taken into captivity and carried into Babylon by King Nebuchadnezzar. For many years, he served as the king's cupbearer. When he learned that Jerusalem had been destroyed and those who remained there were in trouble and were disgraced, he became distraught and prayed to God that He would hear the cries of the people and meet their needs (Nehemiah 1). He then went to the king, asking permission to return to Jerusalem. The book of Nehemiah describes what he found when he got to Jerusalem and how he led the people to rebuild the wall. Throughout the rebuilding, Nehemiah faced criticism, threats of violence, and hard labor. God used Nehemiah's courage, determination, and faith to lead the small band of people remaining in the broken-down city to rebuild the walls and restore security to Jerusalem.

New Testament leaders

The New Testaments introduces God's example of leadership in the life of Jesus. Earlier prophets had described the coming Messiah as a leader of the Israelites. Based on these Old Testament prophecies, the Jewish people were looking for a political or military leader. That may be why most people did not recognize Jesus as the Promised One. He did not come as a leader in the traditional sense. His life was one dedicated to people, meeting needs, encouraging them, and guiding them into a knowledge and faith of His salvation. He was sinless, exhibiting every trait of a godly leader.

Today's leaders would do well to see how Jesus took time to be with people (John 4; Luke 22), how He handled confrontation (Matthew 12; Mark 15), and how He maintained balance in His life (Luke 10:38; Matthew 26:36-44). He made instruction a priority, dedicating time to teaching large groups of people as well as individuals. His heart for people was evident as He spoke with the rich young ruler (Matthew 19:16-30) and the woman caught in adultery (John 8:3-11).

Jesus met people's needs, demonstrated patience with doubters, and lived out His purpose all the way to the cross (John 19:30). He was sensitive to those around Him, recognizing the humanness and frailty of those around Him while expecting and holding them to a high standard (John 6:60-69). The lives of His disciples after His death and resurrection, along with the growth of the early church, attest to the effectiveness of His leadership.

While Jesus is our ultimate example of leadership, let's look at two more human leaders from the New Testament, Peter and Paul. Peter had been with Jesus throughout the three years of His earthly ministry. He had been taught by Jesus and witnessed His healings and miracles. Still, at the first opportunity to stand for Him, Peter failed. He denied Jesus three times in one day (John 18). The remorse and regret Peter felt was overwhelming, but Jesus knew Peter's heart and his potential as a leader. After His resurrection, Jesus appeared specifically to Peter. He reaffirmed His love for His disciple and gave him the assignment, "Feed my sheep" (John 21:15-18). The book of Acts and two books bearing his name attest to Peter's faithfulness to Jesus' instructions. He preached the gospel message to the Jews and provided support to Paul and other missionaries as they witnessed in Gentile nations.

The apostle Paul did not start out as a follower of Jesus. Rather, he is first seen in Acts as a persecutor of the disciples. But in Acts 9, we see that God had other plans for him. Following an amazing conversion experience on his way to Damascus, Paul became the most outspoken and influential leader of the early church. His three missionary journeys resulted in churches across Asia. He experienced many hardships during these trips, including shipwreck, beatings, and attempts on his life. Through his writings, we see that he had a heart for people. He knew people by name and prayed for them daily. He wrote to Timothy, saying,

"I thank God... as night and day I constantly remember you in my prayers. Recalling your tears, I long to see you, so that I may be filled with joy. I am reminded of your sincere faith, which first lived in your grandmother Lois and in your mother Eunice and, I am persuaded, now lives in you also" (2 Timothy 1:3-5).

Our Response to Leadership

What should our response be to those who lead? Does it matter whether they are Christian or not? Does it matter if they are leading well or poorly? Paul wrote to the new church, *"Have confidence in your leaders and submit to their authority, because they keep watch over you as those who must give an account. Do this so that their work will be a joy, not a burden, for that would be of no benefit to you"* (Hebrews 13:17). Notice the word "submit." We saw this same word used earlier when Paul was writing to the Romans. To refresh our memory, let's look at just the first verse of Romans 13, *"Everyone must submit to the governing authorities."* Submission implies obedience without question, in recognition of the authority of the other person. From this, we see that regardless of who the person is, whether we agree with their ideas, or even whether they are believers in Christ, we are instructed to submit to their leadership. We do this in obedience to God and to honor Him.

Does that mean we are to blindly follow someone just because they are in a position of leadership? To understand this better, let's look at a few passages of Scripture. We find the first example in the Old Testament book of Daniel, the story of a young Hebrew man who had been captured in Jerusalem and taken into Babylon as a prisoner. Daniel and a few of his friends were taken into the palace to train to be the king's personal servers. They were given orders regarding food and prayer that went against their religious beliefs. In chapter 1, we read, *"But Daniel made up his mind that he would not defile himself with the king's choice food or with the wine which he drank; so he sought permission from the commander of the officials that he might not defile himself"* (vs 8 [NASB]). What was the outcome? *"Now God granted Daniel favor and compassion in the sight of the commander of the officials"* (vs 9).

In case you think that defying orders always goes smoothly, we need to keep reading. In chapter 3, we find that Daniel's friends were later thrown into a furnace for refusing the king's order to bow before the gold idol he had erected in Babylon. When the king demanded them to bow, these three young men replied:

> *King Nebuchadnezzar, we do not need to defend ourselves before you in this matter. If we are thrown into the blazing furnace, the God we serve is able to deliver us from it, and he will deliver us from Your Majesty's hand. But even if he does not, we want you to know, Your Majesty, that we will not serve your gods or worship the image of gold you have set up"* (vs 16-18).

If you don't know the end of the story, you should read the rest of the chapter. Suffice it to say that God again proved faithful and protected them from the fire.

What about obeying those who claim to be following God? Let's see what Jesus taught His disciples. In Matthew 23, Jesus warned His followers to beware of false religious leaders. He told them:

> *"So you must be careful to do everything they tell you. But do not do what they do, for they do not practice what they preach. They tie up heavy, cumbersome loads and put them on other people's shoulders, but they themselves are not willing to lift a finger to move them. Everything they do is done for people to see: They make their phylacteries wide and the tassels on their garments long; they love the place of honor at banquets and the most important seats in the synagogues; they love to be greeted with respect in the marketplaces and to be called 'Rabbi' by others"* (vs 3-7).

He then pronounced a series of judgments, or "woes," on these ungodly leaders. Finally, he told his disciples:

> *I am sending you out like sheep among wolves. Therefore be as shrewd as snakes and as innocent as doves. Be on your guard; you will be handed over to the local councils and be flogged in the synagogues. On my account you will be brought before governors and kings as witnesses to them and to the Gentiles. But when they arrest you, do not worry about what to say or how to say it. At that time you will be given what to say, for it will not be you speaking, but the Spirit of your Father speaking through you"* (Matthew 10:16-20).

So then, how are we to act? First, we are told to pray for our leaders (1 Timothy 2:1-2). Then, as much as we are able, we are to submit to their authority. We are to obey as an act of obedience to God and to bring honor to Him. When their rules or expectations go directly against our personal beliefs, we are to maintain an attitude of respect, making every attempt to peacefully disagree. As Paul wrote to the early church, *"Remind the people to be subject to rulers and authorities, to be obedient, to be ready to do whatever is good, to slander no one, to be peaceable and considerate, and always to be gentle toward everyone"* (Titus 3:1-2). Always remember that others are watching our response to leadership. May we represent the Christ we serve well.

WEALTH, WELFARE, AND RESOURCES

"Money, Money, Money!!" "Show me the money!" "Money makes the world go 'round." "If I were a rich man…" Do these thoughts come to your mind on a regular basis? If so, you are like most Americans. America is the richest country in the world. Our standard of living far surpasses that of other countries. So why do we still struggle to meet financial demands? Why are we sinking in debt? Why do so many people live in poverty? In order to answer these questions, we need to know what God's Word has to say about wealth. Let's dig in and discover God's formula for wealth.

Biblical Principles Regarding Wealth

Money and wealth are two very common topics in the Bible. We find passages in both the Old and New Testaments that speak to the importance of money in everyday life. Many of the proverbs address the proper attitude towards wealth, as well as warnings against its misuse. Jesus spoke of money as He commented on the widow's mite (Luke 21:1-4) and He reacted decisively to the moneychangers in the temple (Matthew 21:12-13). He even had the disciples retrieve a coin from a fish's mouth to pay their taxes (Matthew 17:24-27). As we seek to live according to God's word, we must have an understanding of His principles regarding this important topic

God is the giver of all things

Before we begin looking at the process of acquiring and using wealth, we must first consider where wealth comes from. God is the Creator of everything; everything belongs to Him and everything we have comes from Him. That includes money, resources, material possessions…everything! Take a look at just a few of the verses clearly stating that God is Creator and the source of everything:

> *You are the Lord, you alone. You have made heaven, the heaven of heavens, with all their host, the earth and all that is on it, the seas and all that is in them; and you preserve all of them; and the host of heaven worships you* (Nehemiah 9:6 [ESV]).

> *Worthy are you, our Lord and God, to receive glory and honor and power, for you created all things, and by your will they existed and were created* (Revelation 4:11 [ESV]).

> *He is the image of the invisible God, the firstborn of all creation. For by him all things were created, in heaven and on earth, visible and invisible, whether thrones or dominions or rulers or authorities—all things were created through him and for him* (Colossians 1:15-16 [ESV]).

> *Every good thing given and every perfect gift is from above, coming down from the Father of lights, with whom there is no variation or shifting shadow"* (James 1:17).

We are stewards of God's world

The word "steward" is seldom used today and most commonly refers to a waiter or airline worker who serves diners or passengers. In the Bible, a steward was someone who had been given the responsibility of caring for someone else's possessions. For example, the owner of a large estate may have designated a person to oversee and manage his property while he was away on an extended trip. This person, or steward, would have made sure that the property was taken care of and that finances were handled properly. The steward would have overseen the estate's employees, ensuring they performed their duties as expected. In naming someone as a steward, the owner was placing trust in this person to carry out this responsibility with integrity and excellence. The Bible highlights several people who acted as stewards. In Genesis 2, God assigned Adam and Eve to be caretakers, or stewards, of His creation. He gave them the responsibility of naming the animals and overseeing them. Later, Joseph served as a steward in Potiphar's house (Genesis 39:1-9). He also served as a steward for Pharaoh, overseeing the distribution of grain during the years of famine (Genesis 41:40-44). Just as God assigned Adam the task of caring for the world He created, we have also been given the same responsibility. As good stewards, we should do our best to carry out this special assignment.

The concept of steward is also presented in the New Testament. Followers of Christ were considered stewards of the gospel, given the responsibility to faithfully share the message of salvation with others as Jesus did when He was on earth. Paul wrote, *"This is how one should regard us, as servants of Christ and stewards of the mysteries… it is required of stewards that they be found trustworthy"* (I Corinthians 4:1-2).

Money and possessions are tools

One particular verse regarding money that is often misquoted or misused is 1 Timothy 6:10. It says, *"For the love of money is a root of all kinds of evils…"* We should note that it is the love of money, not the money itself, that is being described here. The verse also says it is a "root" of all kinds of evils. Money is not evil in and of itself; it is only a tool. Money can be a root, or foundation, for the beginning of evil. We know that many horrendous and evil things are done in an attempt to get money. Robberies, murders, extortion, and exploitation all stem from a desire for money. It is also obvious that money has been used (quite effectively, I might add) to promote evil. Pornography, prostitution, and terrorism are only a few of the ways money is used to promote ungodly values and to bring harm to innocent people.

This brings us back to the original thought. Money and possessions are not evil; they are tools. Margaret Thatcher (1925-2013), first female Prime Minister of Britain, said, "No one would remember the Good Samaritan if he'd only had good intentions; he had money as well."[1] You have the responsibility and discretion to decide how you use your money and possessions. Will it be for good or evil, providing for others or for personal pleasure?

Debt enslaves a person

In our current society, debt is a way of life. For young people, it may be considered a rite of passage to get the first credit card. Student loans are available to nearly every student and the average car is financed for five or more years. While most people view debt as a necessity, the Bible clearly presents a different view. Consider these passages:

> *The rich rules over the poor, and the borrower is the slave of the lender* (Proverbs 22:7 [ESV]).
>
> *Owe no one anything, except to love each other* (Romans 13:8).
>
> *Do not be one who shakes hands in pledge or puts up security for debts; if you lack the means to pay, your very bed will be snatched from under you* (Proverbs 22:26-27).

There is nothing liberating about debt. Even small debt puts the borrower at the mercy of the lender. Being in debt can cause stress, fear, and distrust. It can undermine relationships, particularly when spouses disagree about the use of money. Debt prevents a person from using his income for current needs and limits his ability to plan for the future. The Bible even warns against putting up collateral or co-signing for someone else. Doing this for family or friends may strain the relationship and have lasting repercussions for both parties.

Contentment in all circumstances

Americans today are living in a society that values having the newest and best of everything. Just look at the popularity of the newest iPhone or computer upgrade. In its mild form, this mindset of always wanting more can create feelings of discontent and anxiety. Taken to extremes, we may become consumed by feelings of greed and jealousy that can disrupt everyday life. The Chinese philosopher Lao-Tzu once said, "There is no calamity greater than lavish desires. There is no greater guilt than discontentment. And there is no greater disaster than greed." [2]

The apostle Paul wrote in Philippians 4, *"I have learned to be content whatever the circumstances. I know what it is to be in need, and I know what it is to have plenty. I have learned the secret of being content in any and every situation, whether well fed or hungry, whether living in plenty or in want. I can do all things through Christ who strengthens me" (vs 11-13).*

He later wrote to a young minister and friend that *"godliness with contentment is great gain. For we brought nothing into the world, and we can take nothing out of it. But if we have food and clothing, we will be content with that"* (1 Timothy 6:6-8).

We can't take it with us

People often seem to lose sight of the fact that nothing we have on earth will go with us when we die. We may leave our wealth as an inheritance to those we love, but we will no longer have need of money or possessions. In Matthew 6:19-20, we read *"Do not store up for yourselves treasures on earth, where moth and rust destroy, and where thieves break in and steal. But store up for yourselves treasures in heaven, where neither moth nor rust destroys, and where thieves do not break in or steal."*

Jesus also taught, *"Sell your possessions and give to charity; make yourselves money belts which do not wear out, an unfailing treasure in heaven, where no thief comes near nor moth destroys. For where your treasure is, there your heart will be also"* (Luke 12:33-34).

Godly Attitudes Towards Wealth

We see that God's perspective about money and wealth is quite different from the world's view. The Bible speaks to two very specific attitudes regarding wealth, namely a willingness to work and a willingness to give.

Value hard work

For many people, "work" is a dirty four-letter word, but the Bible teaches that work has value and that everyone who is able should engage in productive work. When we actively engage in work, we have the ability to provide for ourselves and our families, we develop a sense of self-worth, and we have opportunities to serve others. The Holy Spirit has equipped us with skills and talents that we are to use to build up the church and to minister to those around us. Peter reminded the early believers, saying, *"Each of you should use whatever gift you have received to serve others, as faithful stewards of God's grace"* (1 Peter 4:10). Many verses in the Bible describe the type of attitude we should have towards our work:

> *But remember the Lord your God, for it is he who gives you the ability to produce wealth, and so confirms his covenant, which he swore to your ancestors, as it is today* (Deuteronomy 8:18).

> *A slack hand causes poverty, but the hand of the diligent makes rich* (Proverbs 10:4 [ESV]).

> *Wealth gained hastily will dwindle, but whoever gathers little by little will increase it* (Proverbs 13:11 [ESV]).

Prepare your work outside; get everything ready for yourself in the field, and after that build your house (Proverbs 24:27 [ESV]).

Make it your ambition to lead a quiet life and attend to your own business and work with your hands, just as we instructed you (1 Thessalonians 4:11).

Now such persons we command and encourage in the Lord Jesus Christ to do their work quietly and to earn their own living. As for you, brothers, do not grow weary in doing good. If anyone does not obey what we say in this letter, take note of that person, and have nothing to do with him, that he may be ashamed (2 Thessalonians 3:12-14 [ESV]).

Have a generous spirit

The concept of giving to the Lord is introduced in the early chapters of Genesis. In Chapter 4, we read that the Lord looked with favor on Abel's offering. Later, in Chapter 8, Noah presented offerings to thank God for keeping his family safe through the flood. The book of Leviticus introduces the concept of giving one-tenth (a tithe) of our earnings to God. At that time, a "first-fruits" offering was given to the Lord as a sign of recognition that everything comes from Him. It was expected that the first and best of the crops and livestock would be given. Here are just a few of the many verses on tithes and offerings from the Old Testament:

A tithe of everything from the land, whether grain from the soil or fruit from the trees, belongs to the Lord; it is holy to the Lord (Leviticus 27:30).

Every tithe of the herd and flock—every tenth animal that passes under the shepherd's rod—will be holy to the Lord (Leviticus 27:32).

Then to the place the Lord your God will choose as a dwelling for his Name—there you are to bring everything I command you: your burnt offerings and sacrifices, your tithes and special gifts, and all the choice possessions you have vowed to the Lord (Deuteronomy 12:11).

Bring the whole tithe into the storehouse, so that there may be food in my house. Test me in this, says the Lord Almighty, "and see if I do not open for you the floodgates of heaven and pour out so much blessing that there will not be room enough to store it (Malachi 3:10).

In the New Testament, the Jewish people were expected to continue giving tithes and offerings to the Lord. Jesus' teachings did not contradict this expectation, but He was more concerned about a person's attitude toward giving rather than on how much he gave. While at the temple, Jesus watched people bringing their offerings. Luke 21:1-4 describes Jesus' reaction:

Now he looked up and saw the wealthy putting their gifts into the temple treasury. And he saw a poor widow putting in two coins. And he said, "Truly I say to you, this poor widow put in more than all of them; for they all contributed to the offering from their surplus; but she, from her poverty, put in all that she had to live on.

Jesus also taught that we should give generously. In the Sermon on the Mount, He said, *"Give, and it will be given to you. A good measure, pressed down, shaken together and running over, will be poured into your lap. For with the measure you use, it will be measured to you"* (Luke 6:38). When sending out the disciples, Jesus told them, *"Heal the sick, raise the dead, cleanse those who have leprosy, drive out demons. Freely you have received; freely give"* (Matthew 10:8). The apostle Paul reminded the leaders of the church in Ephesus of Jesus' teachings, saying *"In everything I showed you that by working hard in this way you must help the weak and remember the words of the Lord Jesus, that he himself said, 'It is more blessed to give than to receive'"* (Acts 20:35).

One of the saddest stories in the Bible is that of the rich man who came to Jesus. The story is so poignant that it is recorded in three of the four gospels. Matthew, Mark, and Luke described this encounter between a young ruler and Jesus. The rich man knelt before Jesus and asked what he must do in order to inherit eternal life. Jesus first reminded him of the Old Testament commandments, to which the man responded he had done these things since he was a young child. Jesus then said to him, *"Go and sell all you possess and give to the poor, and you will have treasure in heaven. Then come, follow me"* (Mark 10:21). The Bible tells us the young man left Jesus saddened because he owned much property. There may have also been an unwillingness to sacrifice what he had materially in order to receive what Jesus was offering spiritually.

Charles Dickens, in his classic novel, *A Christmas Carol,* introduces the character of Ebenezer Scrooge, a cold-hearted miser who had no interest in Christmas. The term "scrooge" has become associated with stinginess and having an ungenerous spirit. In contrast, Christians are encouraged to develop a generous attitude and give freely of our time, talents, and possessions. Even those who have little in one area may be able to generously share in other ways. For example, someone with limited financial resources may offer his time or skills to help others. As Christians, God has equipped each one of us with something to offer to someone in need. Consider these verses to help stretch your generous spirit:

> *However, since we have gifts that differ according to the grace given to us, each of us is to use them properly… if service, in the act of serving; or the one who teaches, in the act of teaching; or the one who exhorts, in the work of exhortation; the one who gives, with generosity* (Romans 12:6-8).

> *So I considered it necessary to urge the brothers that they go on ahead to you and arrange in advance your previously promised generous gift, that the same would be ready as a generous gift, and not as one grudgingly given due to greediness. Now I say this: the one who sows sparingly will also reap sparingly, and the one who sows generously will also reap generously. Each one must do just as he has decided in his heart, not*

reluctantly or under compulsion, for God loves a cheerful giver (2 Corinthians 9:5-7).

Let love of the brothers and sisters continue. Do not neglect hospitality to strangers, for by this some have entertained angels without knowing it (Hebrews 13:1-3).

Through him then, let's continually offer up a sacrifice of praise to God, that is, the fruit of lips praising his name. And do not neglect doing good and sharing, for with such sacrifices God is pleased (Hebrews 13: 15-16).

Attitudes to Avoid

While we are working to develop positive, godly attitudes towards wealth and possessions, we are also warned of several attitudes to avoid. Let's look at a few attitudes that can undermine our Christian character and witness.

Laziness: I saw a t-shirt the other day that read, "I may be up and dressed, but that doesn't mean I'm ready to do things." If I am being totally honest, laziness is one of the biggest hurdles I face on a daily basis. Putting something off until tomorrow is so much easier than doing it today. The Bible's word for laziness is "slothfulness" and a lazy person is referred to as a "sluggard." Neither of these words sound appealing to me. The book of Proverbs contains many warnings to avoid laziness:

Poor is one who works with a lazy hand, But the hand of the diligent makes rich (Proverbs 10:4).

The soul of the sluggard craves and gets nothing, while the soul of the diligent is richly supplied (Proverbs 13:4 [ESV]).

The lazy one buries his hand in the dish, but will not even bring it back to his mouth (Proverbs 19:24).

The lazy one does not plow after the autumn, So he begs during the harvest and has nothing (Proverbs 20:4).

The desire of the lazy one puts him to death, For his hands refuse to work… (Proverbs 21:25).

The apostle Paul also wrote a strong admonition to the new Christians at Thessalonica. Second Thessalonians 3:10 (ESV) reads, *"For even when we were with you, we would give you this command: If anyone is not willing to work, let him not eat."* Later in that same letter, he wrote, *"And we urge you, brothers, admonish the idle, encourage the fainthearted, help the weak, and be patient with them all"* (1 Thessalonians 5:14 ESV). And to Timothy, he wrote, *"It is the hard-working farmer who ought to have the first share of the crops"* (2 Timothy 2:6 [ESV]).

<u>Arrogance and Pride:</u> One of the by-products of wealth is power and prestige. In general, wealthy people are often in positions of leadership and influence in today's society. Along with the responsibility that comes with this status, we must guard against developing attitudes of arrogance and pride. I am not talking about the type of pride we feel when we have done a job well or when we see our children succeeding. Those feelings are appropriate and healthy. Instead, what we should avoid are arrogance and pride that suggest that we are better than others. This type of pride is boastful and self-indulgent, with the purpose of getting attention while belittling others. When we don't recognize that everything we obtained or accomplished is through God's power, it is easy to become boastful. When Moses was leading the Israelites into the Promised Land, he gave them this warning:

Beware that you do not forget the Lord your God by not keeping his commandments and his ordinances and his statutes which I am commanding you today; otherwise, when you have eaten and are satisfied, and have built good houses and lived in them, and when your herds and your flocks multiply, and your silver and gold multiply, and all that you have multiplies, then your heart will become proud and you will forget the Lord your God who brought you out from the land of Egypt, out of the house of slavery (Deuteronomy 8:11-14).

Jesus also taught about arrogance and pride. He warned His disciples to not imitate the religious leaders, saying, *"Take care not to practice your righteousness in the sight of people, to be noticed by them; otherwise you have no reward with your Father who is in heaven. So when you give to the poor, do not sound a trumpet before you, as the hypocrites do in the synagogues and on the streets, so that they will be praised by people. Truly I say to you, they have their reward in full"* (Matthew 6:1-2).

Greed: Earlier, we looked at developing a generous spirit. The opposite of generosity is greed. Merriam-Webster defines "greed" as "a selfish and excessive desire for more of something (such as money) than is needed."[3] Jesus clearly stated that love of wealth is a false god (Matthew 6:24; Luke 16:13). 1 John 2:15 warns us, *"Do not love the world or the things in this world."* Desire for material possessions, wealth, and fame, while not necessarily bad in moderation, may compete with God for our devotion and become a modern-day form of idolatry.[4]

One of the worst things about greed is that it tends to cause people to consider actions that may hurt others. The Bible warns about taking advantage of those in need, speaking out specifically about the greed of charging interest on loans to others. Here are just a few verses dealing with the topic of interest:

If you lend money to one of my people among you who is needy, do not treat it like a business deal; charge no interest (Exodus 22:25).

Do not take any kind of interest from him, but fear your God, so that your countryman may live with you. You shall not give him your silver at interest, nor your food for profit (Leviticus 25: 36-37).

Whoever increases wealth by taking interest or profit from the poor amasses it for another, who will be kind to the poor (Proverbs 28:8).

Charity

Many of us at some time or other will find ourselves in need of assistance. We may lose a job, experience illness, or need food or housing. Natural disasters such as floods and tornados may put people in need without warning. Others may find themselves in relationships and situations that are unsafe. Regardless of the cause, we are called as Christians to have sensitive and caring hearts towards those in need. We are called to see each person as God sees them – unique, special, and loved. When Jesus was asked about the greatest commandment, He said, *"'You shall love the Lord your God with all your heart, and with all your soul, and with all your mind.' This is the great and greatest commandment."* He added, *"The second is like it, 'You shall love your neighbor as yourself'"* (Matthew 22:37-39). Charity is defined as "generosity and helpfulness especially toward the needy or suffering; aid given to those in need."[5] Christians are called to give to others in verses such as, *"Give to him who asks of you, and do not turn away from him who wants to borrow from you"* (Matthew 5:42) and, *"Whoever has worldly goods and sees his brother or sister in need, and closes his heart against him, how does the love of God remain in him?"* (1 John 3:17).

In the Old Testament, as the Israelites were becoming a nation, God gave Moses clear instructions on how people should act towards each other. The following passage highlights what God expects from us in how we care for others:

> *If there is a poor person among you, one of your brothers, in any of your towns in your land which the Lord your God is giving you, you shall not harden your heart, nor close your hand from your poor brother; but you shall fully open your hand to him, and generously lend him enough for his need in whatever he lacks. Be careful that there is no mean-spirited thought in your heart, such as, 'The seventh year, the year of release of debts, is near,' and your eye is malicious toward your poor brother, and you give him nothing; then he may cry out to the Lord against you, and it will be a sin in you. You shall generously give to him, and your heart*

shall not be grudging when you give to him, because for this thing the Lord your God will bless you in all your work, and in all your undertakings. For the poor will not cease to exist in the land; therefore I am commanding you, saying, 'You shall fully open your hand to your brother, to your needy and poor in your land' (Deuteronomy 15:7-11).

The Bible clearly states that we are to love, minister to, and support those in need. Further, God promises to bless those who bless others. Proverbs 14:21 tells us, *"One who despises his neighbor sins, But one who is gracious to the poor is blessed."* Isaiah beautifully describes the blessings God bestows on those who show charity:

If you spend yourselves in behalf of the hungry and satisfy the needs of the oppressed, then your light will rise in the darkness, and your night will become like the noonday. The Lord will guide you always; He will satisfy your needs in a sun-scorched land and will strengthen your frame. You will be like a well-watered garden, like a spring whose waters never fail (Isaiah 58: 10-11).

As we become aware of those around us, we can easily become overwhelmed by the sheer number of people in need. How do we determine who should receive our charity? Luke 10:29-37 tells the familiar story of the Good Samaritan. In this parable, Jesus gives a vivid picture of charity in action. We are not told the social or financial status of the man who was attacked by robbers; we are merely told that he was hurt and in need of assistance. Although others, namely a priest and a Levite, see the injured man and pass him by, the Samaritan, seeing the man's need, offers his time and money without expecting anything in return.

Besides helping the injured or ill, the Bible gives us several other specific groups of people we are called to help. They most likely have little to no means of providing for themselves and, at least for a short time, require assistance from others. The following verses identify orphans, widows, those who have fallen on hard times, and foreigners or strangers as among those who should be given aid:

> *Religion that is pure and holy before God is this: to visit orphans and widows in their affliction* (James 1:27).

> *Now in case a countryman of yours becomes poor and his means among you falter, then you are to sustain him, like a stranger or a resident, so that he may live with you* (Leviticus 25:35).

> *Now when you reap the harvest of your land, you shall not reap to the very edges of your field, nor shall you gather the gleanings of your harvest. And you shall not glean your vineyard, nor shall you gather the fallen grapes of your vineyard; you shall leave them for the needy and for the stranger* (Leviticus 19:9-10).

Welfare

Welfare, the concept of seeking the general health and happiness of others, has been around for thousands of years. During the 1930s, under President Franklin D. Roosevelt's leadership, a formal program for providing welfare was formed. This federal welfare program was established to provide support for those who were unemployed, children, and dependents.[6] Today, in addition to Social Security income for retirees, welfare provides medical coverage and food programs for millions of Americans. Programs support the disabled, low-income seniors, and mothers and families with children. For many, these programs provide necessary support during times of financial difficulty. For others, they become a way of life.

What does the Bible have to say about welfare? For starters, welfare should be only for those who have no other means of support. In 1 Timothy 5, the apostle Paul gave Timothy specific instructions about assisting widows. For example, in verse 4, he noted that if a widow has family, they should provide for her. He also warned against putting younger widows who might remarry on the list for assistance (vs 11). Finally, he wrote, *"No widow may be put on the list of widows unless she is over sixty, has been faithful to her husband, and is well known for her good deeds, such as bringing up children, showing hospitality, washing the feet of the Lord's people, helping those in trouble and devoting herself to all kinds of good deeds"* (vs 9-10). How many people would that eliminate from our current welfare rolls?

Work is a common theme throughout the Bible. We are told in Exodus 20:9, *"Six days you shall work and do all your labor."* The writer of Ecclesiastes tells us that we should consider our work to be a gift from God (5:19). Paul warned fellow believers not to tolerate idleness. He wrote:

Now we command you, brothers, in the name of our Lord Jesus Christ, that you keep away from any brother who is walking in idleness and not in accord with the tradition that you received from us. For you yourselves know how you ought to imitate us, because we were not idle when we were with you, nor did we eat anyone's bread without paying for it, but with toil and labor we worked night and day, that we might not be a burden to any of you. It was not because we do not have that right, but to give you in ourselves an example to imitate. For even when we were with you, we would give you this command: If anyone is not willing to work, let him not eat (2 Thessalonians 3:6-12).

I admit that these are strong words. John Hagee summarized this idea in a rather bold way, saying, "Simply stated, if you can work, work or starve to death."[7] Obviously, this applies to those who have the ability to work. For those who do not have the ability to work or in rare circumstances where no work is available, we should be willing to meet their needs while encouraging them to look for other ways to be productive. Much of a person's dignity and sense of worth comes from work, being self-sufficient and able to provide for his family. When a person's opportunity and incentive to work are taken away, pride and self-esteem are lost. When we are seeking the best for a person, it is imperative that they be encouraged and expected to work in any way they can.

Finally, we must recognize that being generous with time and money does not mean that we are obligated to give to people who are clearly not in need or who just want to take advantage of us. The apostle Paul wrote, *"We hear that some among you are idle and disruptive. They are not busy; they are busybodies. Such people we command and urge in the Lord Jesus Christ to settle down and earn the food they eat. And as for you, brothers and sisters, never tire of doing what is good"* (2 Thessalonians 3:11-13).

Natural Resources

Finally, let's examine what the Bible says about natural resources. As we have previously discussed, God is the Creator of everything and man is blessed with the fruits of His creation. In Genesis 9, God told Adam, *"Every moving thing that lives shall be food for you. And as I gave you the green plants, I give you everything"* (vs 3). And we have discussed our responsibility to be good stewards and care for His creation. Psalm 8 reminds us:

> *When I consider your heavens, the work of your fingers,*
> *the moon and the stars, which you have set in place,*
> *what is mankind that you are mindful of them,*
> *human beings that you care for them?*
> *You have made them a little lower than the angels*
> *and crowned them with glory and honor.*
> *You made them rulers over the works of your hands;*
> *You put everything under their feet:*
> *all flocks and herds, and the animals of the wild,*
> *the birds in the sky, and the fish in the sea,*
> *all that swim the paths of the seas.*
> *Lord, our Lord, how majestic is your name in all the earth!*
> (vs 3-9)

The Old Testament concept of the Year of Jubilee provides an example of this responsibility. Leviticus 25 presents the instructions God gave the Israelites to observe the Year of Jubilee. Every seven years, the land was to be returned to its original owner. This ensured that the original family would retain ownership of the land given by Moses. The Year of Jubilee reminds us that we don't have ownership of things. Instead, we only have use of it for a time. Leviticus 25:23 (ESV) states, *"The land shall not be sold in perpetuity, for the land is mine. For you are strangers and sojourners with me."* As stewards, we are not to neglect or destroy the resources we have. Reasonable effort should be made to preserve our natural resources. For example, the Israelites were told that the land could be cultivated and reaped for six years but should be allowed to rest during the seventh year. In effect, this would be a Sabbath for the land. Why should they do this? God said, *"Follow my decrees and be careful to obey my laws, and you will live safely in the land. Then the land will yield its fruit, and you will eat your fill and live there in safety"* (Leviticus 25: 18-19). Basically, God was saying, "If you will take care of my world, then I will take care of you."

Some people believe that man has the ability to destroy the world through the misuse of resources and that the world will end because of global climate changes. They promote an attitude of fear. But the Bible tells us more than 365 times, "Fear not!" Following the flood that destroyed the earth, God told Noah, *"While the earth remains, seedtime and harvest, cold and heat, summer and winter, day and night, shall not cease"* (Genesis 8:22). Avery Foley, writer and cohost of the *Answers in Genesis* broadcast, commented on this passage:

> God has promised that we will continue to have seasons and that we will continue to be able to grow food. Will climate change? Absolutely. It has in the past, and it will change in the future. That may close off some areas to agriculture but may open up new areas we currently cannot use. But even as the climate changes, we can know the predictable seasons will

continue, even if they don't look quite how they looked to previous generations living in a particular area.[8]

We do not need to live in a spirit of fear. Instead, let us remain thankful for all God has given us and ask for His wisdom in using our wealth and resources for His glory!

Part 2 Chapter 4

MARRIAGE AND FAMILY

Scientists have identified six elements that are the basic "building blocks of life," namely, hydrogen, carbon, nitrogen, oxygen, phosphorus, and sulfur. These elements are essential for life. Similarly, educators have identified three building blocks of learning – reading, writing, and arithmetic. When children have acquired these skills, they are able to master more advanced material and continue learning on their own. The Bible tells us, in the same way, that God ordained the family to be the primary building block of society. He created the family with the intention that within this unit, relationships would be formed, problems solved, wisdom shared, and values taught. Children would learn how to live according to God's plan from adults serving as role models. However, today's culture is drastically changing the definition of "family." Society now identifies any group of people living together as a family, granting them the same rights and protections as those from traditional families.

When God's concept of family is compromised, however, every aspect of the family is affected. The foundation becomes shaky, unity is torn, support is missing, and godly training is abandoned. Strong families develop members who are confident and competent to contribute to society, and who in turn, can raise future generations of strong families.

A casual glance at society reveals that no two families are alike. There are families with many children and families with no children, blended families and single-parent families. There are families experiencing illness, addiction, and abuse. There are families where individuals live with feelings of resentment, anger, and loneliness. Many children are being raised by grandparents or in foster homes.

Multi-generational families are common among many cultural groups, whereas in urban areas, many adults live distanced from family.

Some families function well, despite the circumstances they face, while others are adversely affected. Family dysfunction is not a modern concept. Genesis, the first book of the Bible, contains many examples of dysfunctional families. Sibling rivalry existed between Cain and Abel, Jacob and Esau, as well as between Joseph and his brothers. Jacob's father-in-law, Laban, deceived him on his wedding day by secretly replacing the bride Jacob was promised with her older sister. Lot's daughters, to bear children who would continue the family name, acted to get him intoxicated and had sex with him. King Saul hated his son for supporting David. Some of these situations sound like episodes of reality television.

I realize that no one gets to choose the family he is born into and if your family resembles some of those mentioned earlier, please know that this chapter is not intended to pass judgment on you or those you love or to criticize any particular form of "family." My goal is to describe the type of family God desires for us and can bless. While the Bible clearly states specific "do's and "don'ts," God doesn't give us these laws to attack us or make us feel guilty. He doesn't give them so that we can criticize and blame those who follow different paths. Let's not put blinders on and lose focus of the larger picture. We need to examine these commands in light of God's perfect love for His people. God, in His infinite wisdom, knows what is best for us. His laws help us live a life that will bring joy, happiness, and a blessed future for us, our families, and our nation.

God's Plan for the Family

Source of support, help, and encouragement

One of the first things God did after creating the world was to create man. This first man, Adam, was formed *"in God's image"* (Genesis

1:27). He placed Adam as caretaker of His garden. Recognizing that Adam had a big responsibility and that he was alone, God formed the first woman as a helper for him. Genesis 2 tells us:

> *The Lord God said, 'It is not good for the man to be alone. I will make a helper suitable for him.'... Then the Lord God made a woman from the rib He had taken out of the man, and He brought her to the man. The man said, 'This is now bone of my bones and flesh of my flesh; she shall be called 'woman,' for she was taken out of man.' That is why a man leaves his father and mother and is united to his wife, and they become one flesh."* (vs 18, 22-24)

Eve was created to be a companion, helper, and friend to Adam. God ordained this union, forming the family as a source of support, help and encouragement.

My husband and I have been married nearly forty years. We are very different in our personalities, interests, and skills. We come from different backgrounds. He grew up in a military family, while my parents were educators. Yet despite our differences (and maybe even because of them), we have worked together as a team in building a home, raising a family, and running a business. We have supported each other through the loss of parents, ill health, and financial challenges. We have guided and encouraged our children through the ups and downs of adolescence and young adulthood. After all we have gone through together, I can honestly say that Chris and I are still best friends. Our children love each other and know, as a family, that we "have each other's backs." We are committed and available to each other. To the outside world, this commitment may seem strange.

When my daughter was a teenager, she complained that our family was weird. She was frustrated that we were more strict than other parents and expressed that she thought some of the things we did were wrong. She was critical that we weren't like her friends' families. I took her comparison as a compliment and waited for her to mature in her attitude. Several years later, we were talking in my kitchen and she mentioned her previous critical commentary. She said that she now appreciates the fact that our family is different. Our support and commitment to each other stands in sharp contrast to many in today's world.

Procreation

The second purpose God has for the family is to have children, thereby ensuring that mankind will continue to exist. The old-fashioned term is "procreation." As people grow old and die, children are born to continue the human race. This is the cycle of life that God ordained when He told the children of Israel to *"be fruitful and multiply."* In Psalms 127:3-5, we read, *"Children are a heritage from the Lord, offspring a reward from him. Like arrows in the hands of a warrior are children born in one's youth. Blessed is the man whose quiver is full of them."* While it is true that not every couple should, can, or will have children, having children is part of God's plan.

Raising future godly generations

Ronald Reagan said, "Freedom is a fragile thing and it's never more than one generation away from extinction. It is not ours by way of inheritance; it must be fought for and defended constantly by each generation."[1] In the same way, we are never more than one generation away from a godless society. God's plan for the family is to raise up the next generation to know and follow Him. The Bible tells us to pass on our Christian heritage and beliefs to our children. The psalmist wrote:

He decreed statutes for Jacob and established the law in Israel, which he commanded our ancestors to teach their children, so the next generation would know them, even the children yet to be born, and they in turn would tell their children. Then they would put their trust in God and would not forget his deeds but would keep his commands" (Psalm 78:5-7).

Proverbs 22:6 (RSV) tells us to *"train up a child in the way he should go and when he is old, he will not depart from it."* In Deuteronomy 32:7, we are advised to seek the wisdom of our elders. *"Remember the days of old; consider the generations long past. Ask your father and he will tell you, your elders, and they will explain to you."*

God is interested in the welfare of our current generation but He also is concerned for all of the generations who will come after us. The word "generation" is used more than 150 times in the Bible. Many of these verses point to blessings and curses that extend to future generations. The field of medicine recognizes the impacts of familial health and disease. The field of psychology recognizes the effects of generational mental illness and dysfunctionality. In the same way, the Bible points out that we are to be responsible for raising and training the next generation to love the Lord and follow His ways.

Picture of God's relationship with His children

A fourth purpose for the family is to provide a tangible expression of the relationship God wants to have with us. God is called "Father" and we are "His children." For those who grew up in difficult family situations, this relationship is hard to grasp. Children who have been hurt or abandoned by their fathers have trouble seeing God the Father as good, kind, and loving. They have a hard time trusting that He wants the best for them, but when a family functions as God intends, we clearly see relationships in which people put the needs of others ahead of their own needs. We see people who love us despite our short-comings and failures, and we see people generously forgive us when we mess up. We see parents giving the best to their children, while loving them enough to discipline them. This is the relationship God wants to have with us. Jesus said, *"If you then, who are evil, know how to give good gifts to your children, how much more will the heavenly Father give the*

Holy Spirit to those who ask him!" (Luke 11:13). He loves us unconditionally. He desires the best for us. In fact, He loves us so much that He sent Jesus to die so that we would have life eternal with Him (John 3:16-17).

Marriage Relationship

Relationships do not succeed on auto-pilot. They take work and intentionality of focus. They require sensitivity and compassion. The marriage relationship is no exception. God has planned this special union to be grounded in several key concepts.

One man and one woman: Billy Graham spoke about marriage, saying, "Nothing brings more joy than a good marriage, and nothing brings more misery than a bad marriage."[2] The Bible tells us that there are several factors necessary for a good and godly marriage. First, God ordained that marriage is designed for one man to be united with one woman. Genesis 2:24 (ESV) states, *"Therefore a man shall leave his father and his mother and hold fast to his wife, and they shall become one flesh."* Until recently, this idea was accepted without debate. Now, the definition of marriage has been expanded to include same-sex marriage. This goes in direct opposition to scripture.

For life: Second, marriage is intended to be for life. When Jesus was asked about marriage and divorce, He quoted Genesis 2:24 and added, *"...so they are no longer two but one flesh. What therefore God has joined together, let no one separate"* (Mark 10:6-9). The apostle Paul taught the new believers in Corinth about God's plan regarding marriage and divorce. He told them, *"To the married I give this charge (not I, but the Lord): the wife must not separate from her husband (but if she does, she should remain unmarried or else be reconciled to her husband), and the husband must not divorce his wife"* (1 Corinthians 7:10-11).

Many people enter marriage with an "opt-out" plan. Modern wedding vows include the phrase "to have and to hold as long as we have love." Young couples casually talk about marriage, saying that if things get tough they will just divorce. I have news for them, marriage is always tough! Challenges and problems will come. Count on it. Expect it. Deal with it and keep your commitment to your spouse.

Authority within the family: God's view of the husband-wife relationship is not a democracy. It is not a 50-50 proposition. I have heard of couples who evenly divide everything from chores to checkbooks. Some couples maintain separate sleeping arrangements, take separate vacations, and even keep the laundry separate. I do not believe this was God's intention when He said they will *become one flesh.*" The unity of one flesh is difficult to achieve when people maintain this level of separation.

God's plan for marriage is for the husband and wife to love each other as they love themselves. Further, they are to love their spouse as Jesus loves His church. This is a sacrificial love that is willing to put the needs and desires of someone else above personal needs. When each partner has this type of love for the other, there is no need to fear power struggles or betrayal. Neither partner dominates the other in a harsh or manipulative manner. Decisions are made that are in the best interest of the family, accommodating the unique needs of individuals within the family.

The Bible provides a plan of authority within the family by describing the relationship that exists between God, Jesus, and the church. God's order of authority flows from Him to the husband and then to his wife. The apostle Paul wrote 1 Corinthians 11, *"But I want you to understand that the head of every man is Christ, the head of a wife is her husband, and the head of Christ is God"* (v 3). Paul later described this relationship, saying:

> *Husbands, love your wives, just as Christ loved the church and gave himself up for her to make her holy, cleansing her by the washing with water through the word, and to present her to himself as a radiant church, without stain or wrinkle or any other blemish, but holy and blameless. In this same way, husbands ought to love their wives as their own bodies.*

He who loves his wife loves himself. After all, no one ever hated their own body, but they feed and care for their body, just as Christ does the church- for we are members of his body (Ephesians 5:25-31).

Paul also spoke directly to wives, urging them to "...*submit yourselves to your own husbands as you do to the Lord. For the husband is the head of the wife as Christ is the head of the church, his body, of which he is the Savior. Now as the church submits to Christ, so also wives should submit to their husbands in everything*" (Ephesians 5:22-24). Reasons for this role of submission are provided in other New Testament passages. 1 Peter 3:1 says that by adopting a posture of submission, unbelieving husbands may be won for the Lord. Titus 2:5 encourages submission so that the Word will not be maligned.

Some people argue that these commands were based on the culture of Bible times and are not applicable or even appropriate for today. I would argue that while women's roles have changed and opportunities available to them have increased, there still exists a need for a hierarchy of authority within the family unit. When God's plan of authority is honored in the family, that family gives honor to God. As a result, He is able to shower the family with His blessings.

Over the course of our marriage, Chris and I have made thousands of decisions, from simple things like what to have for dinner or what television show to watch, to more important things like how many children to have or where to live. We easily agreed on most things. Occasionally, situations arose where the right decision was not clear, where we had different opinions on a topic. Because we had (and still have) a deep love and respect for each other, we were able to talk through these differences without anger or disrespect. Sometimes, we agreed on his idea. Other times, we went with my idea. I would dare to say that most of the decisions we made were compromises. Regardless of the outcome, we recognized that God had given my husband the authority and responsibility to make the final family decision. Chris knows that while I often have good ideas and strong feelings about things, God holds him ultimately accountable for the decisions and actions of our family. Just as Jesus desires to present the church to God as holy and radiant, Chris wants to be able to stand before God one day knowing that he did all he could to have a God-centered marriage and to raise his children to follow Jesus.

Harmony and fulfillment: Psychologists have long known that people have an innate need for relationships with people who love them. American psychologist Abraham Maslow (1908-1970) identified love and belonging as one of man's fundamental needs, along with other needs such as physiological needs, safety needs, esteem, and self-actualization.[3] The Bible tells us that man was created for fellowship with God. After he created Adam, God recognized that Adam needed someone else to share the responsibility he had been given. Eve was to be a helper and companion.

God designed the marriage relationship between a husband and a wife to be harmonious and that each person, through this relationship, would experience happiness and fulfillment. Ecclesiastes 4:9-10 describes this symbiotic relationship, saying, *"Two are better than one, because they have a good return for their labor: If either of them falls down, one can help the other up."*

In this current culture of easy divorce and the mantra "every man for himself," relationships are often used for personal gain, to escape undesired circumstances, and as a means for achieving status in society. Relationships formed for these reasons don't last. They do not look out for the interests of the other person and do not lead to fulfillment. Only relationships built on God's principles have the endurance, joy, and fulfillment He promises.

Godly sexuality: The topic of sexuality has become commonplace in our society. Once taboo, discussions centered on sex occur daily on television, in movies, and even in our workplaces. Vivid portrayals of sex are available with just the click of a computer mouse. So where does God's concept of sexuality fit in? Are the terms "sex" and "love" interchangeable? If God created the concept of sex, can having sex be sinful? Pastor John Ritenbaugh responds, "Humanists have managed to convince men and women that sex and love are the same... that sex and love are one with each other. This is a major departure from what was formerly believed, and it is untrue. Love is so much greater and more important than sex there is no adequate comparison."[4] With that being said, let's look at God's plan for sexuality.

The Bible makes it clear that sexuality within a marriage relationship is not sinful. In Genesis, we are told that Adam and Eve experienced sexual unity without sin. *"Both the man and his wife were naked and they felt no shame"* (Genesis 2:25). The Old Testament book, Song of Songs, describes the intimate relationship between a groom and his bride. When the sexual relationship takes place within the confines of the marriage as God ordained, it serves a three-fold purpose. The first purpose is to bring pleasure to the couple. Within the marriage relationship, God intends for sex to be a wonderful experience between a husband and wife. In his letter to the church at Corinth, Paul wrote, *"Each man should have sexual relations with his own wife, and each woman with her own husband. The husband should fulfill his marital duty to his wife, and likewise the wife to her husband"* (1 Corinthians 7:2-3).

The second purpose of sexual intimacy is to deepen the bond between a man and his wife. *"That is why a man leaves his father and mother and is united to his wife, and they become one flesh"* (Genesis 2:24). Within this exclusive relationship, the couple is free to develop a special intimacy that is not shared with others. They feel open to exposing their faults and failures, knowing that they will find understanding and support rather than criticism and condemnation. And they are free to meet the physical and emotional needs of their spouse. There is no other human relationship where a person can find such total intimacy.

A third purpose of sexual intimacy is to produce offspring. God commanded Adam to *"be fruitful and multiply"* (Genesis 1:28). After the flood, Noah was instructed to *"populate the earth abundantly and multiply in it"* (Genesis 9:7[NASB]). Throughout the Bible, God recognized children as being an inheritance from Him. As Christian parents, we are called to follow the principles of godly parenting discussed earlier in this chapter.

As you can see, God desires that we have a fulfilling sexual relationship with our spouse but God's attitude towards sexual relations outside of marriage is equally clear – He condemns it. Sex before marriage damages future relationships, while adultery damages current relationships. Let's take a closer look at what God's Word tells us about these two types of relationships.

First, let's examine sexual relationships before marriage. Current trends indicate that a majority of people have had at least one sexual relationship before marriage. Why is this a problem? Obvious answers would include unwanted pregnancies, sexually transmitted diseases, and a reputation for promiscuity. Lance Ponder wrote, "When the barriers of moral absolutes are removed, whatever form of pleasure a person desires becomes permissible...Shame ceases to hold us back... there should be no wonder why so many children get pregnant in middle school and all other forms of sexual deviancy are so widely accepted."[5]

However, there are other, more subtle, effects of premarital sex. These center around God's expectations and plans for us and our future spouses. The apostle Paul was explicit in his instruction to the early Christians regarding sex outside of marriage. He wrote in Romans 12:1, *"I urge you, brothers and sisters, in view of God's mercy, to offer your bodies as a living sacrifice, holy and pleasing to God—this is your true and proper worship."* Later, he wrote to the Corinthians:

> *Flee from sexual immorality. All other sins a person commits are outside the body, but whoever sins sexually, sins against their own body. Do you not know that your bodies are temples of the Holy Spirit, who is in you, whom you have received from God? You are not your own; you were bought at a price. Therefore honor God with your bodies*
> (1 Corinthians 6:18-20).

Even before marriage, both the man's and the woman's body belong to their future spouses. In his book, *I Kissed Dating Goodbye*, Joshua Harris emphasizes the deep significance of physical intimacy, noting that God designed sexuality within the marriage relationship. He writes, "A husband and wife may enjoy each other's bodies because they in essence belong to each other. But if you're not married to someone, you have no claim on that person's body, no right to sexual intimacy."[6]

Extramarital sexual relationships bring a new set of challenges. Sex outside the sacred boundaries of marriage creates chaos, pain, and hurt. It undermines the family unit and creates stresses that God never intended. Proverbs 5-7 are dedicated to warning readers about the destruction that adultery can bring. Jesus taught about adultery, saying, *"You have heard that it was said, 'You shall not commit adultery.' But I tell you that anyone who looks at a woman lustfully has already committed adultery with her in his heart"* (Matthew 5:27-28). Jesus also said, *"For it is from within, out of a person's heart, that evil thoughts come—sexual immorality, theft, murder, adultery, greed, malice, deceit, lewdness, envy, slander, arrogance and folly. All these evils come from inside and defile a person"* (Mark 7:21-23).

No chapter on sexuality would be complete without discussing the topic of homosexuality. Society's focus on inclusion and acceptance are at odds with God's plans. In the Old Testament, we read, *"If a man lies with a male as with a woman, both of them have committed an abomination"* (Leviticus 20:13). In the New Testament, Paul writes, *"Do not be deceived: Neither the sexually immoral nor idolaters nor adulterers nor men who have sex with men nor thieves nor the greedy nor drunkards nor slanderers nor swindlers will inherit the kingdom of God"* (1 Corinthians 6:9-10).

There is no ambiguity in the scriptures. Again, we must remember that these commandments are not designed to be punitive but are for our good. We must also remember that while God hates the sin, He loves the sinner. And in fact, we are all sinners. (Romans 3:23)

Raising Children

One of the most rewarding aspects of marriage is the raising of children. New parents experience delight in the birth of a child, enjoying watching him grow and dreaming about his future. As children mature, parents move from being "need-meeters" (my own term) to being "mentors." Watching children become happy and successful adults is one of the greatest joys parents share. I would like to discuss two concepts related to raising children that I believe are significant for our current culture.

<u>Instruction and Training:</u> During the pandemic of recent years, parents were called on to oversee their child's virtual education. I would wager that for most parents, this was an eye-opening experience that gave them a greater appreciation for our nation's teachers. At the same time, however, many parents recognize that our nation's educational system has many shortcomings.

God's word tells parents that they are responsible for the education of their children, regardless of whether they are in public, private, or home-school settings. As such, it is imperative that we remain diligent in monitoring what our children are learning from others and speak up when schools (public or private) teach content that opposes what you know to be truth.

In addition to academic education, parents are also held accountable for instructing their children in social and spiritual matters. Ephesians 6:4 says, *"Fathers, do not exasperate your children; instead, bring them up in the training and instruction of the Lord."* In Deuteronomy, we read, *"Only be careful, and watch yourselves closely so that you do not forget the things your eyes have seen or let them fade from your heart as long as you live. Teach them to your children and to their children after them"* (4:9). Later, we are told to *"...teach them to your children, talking about them when you sit at home and when you walk along the road, when you lie down and when you get up"* (Deuteronomy 11:19).

God has given parents the awesome and daunting task of raising the next generation. Make time to share with your children what you are learning about God, his Son, Jesus, and the purpose He has for you and your family. Set daily times for Bible reading, devotions, and prayer with your kids. Encourage family members to memorize Scripture verses so that God's Word will be *"hidden in their hearts"* (Psalm 119:11). Be available and able to answer their questions about life from a Christian perspective, and by all means, set an example for your children of how a believer in Jesus lives in the current culture.

Discipline: There are many books, websites, podcasts, and blogs that teach parenting skills. Some advocate a strict, disciplinarian approach, while others recommend a more lenient approach in which the parent becomes more of a friend than a parent. The Bible presents parenting in the context of "training" a child. Proverbs 22:6 says to *"train up a child in the way he should go"* (NASB). Training involves more than "telling." It involves teaching and modeling, not just once, but multiple times. It involves discipline and correction done with love.

Proverbs 29:15 states, *"...the rod and reproof give wisdom, but a child left to himself brings shame to his mother"* (ESV). Later in verse 17, the writer says, *"Discipline your son, and he will give you rest; he will give delight to your heart."*

Merriam-Webster offers two definitions for the word "discipline." Most people immediately think of the first definition: to punish or penalize for the sake of enforcing obedience and perfecting moral character. The Biblical concept of discipline is more closely aligned with the second meaning: to train or develop by instruction and exercise, especially in self-control.[7]

Most people, even non-Christians, know the adage, "Spare the rod and spoil the child." They assume this is a direct quote from the Bible. However, the actual verse says, *"Whoever spares the rod hates their children, but the one who loves their children is careful to discipline them"* (Proverbs 13:24). The rod referred to in this verse is not an instrument of pain, but of direction. In Bible times, a shepherd used his rod in many ways, to guide his sheep, to reach for them if they fell into a hole or down the mountainside, and to fight off animals seeking to attack the sheep.

The rod was a means of provision and protection. In the same way, the discipline we provide our children is not designed to harm them, but to guide them towards what is best for them. One word of caution: Parents should remain aware that any act of discipline that is done for punishment or power is not pleasing to God.

Marriage and Family Under Attack

God has told us through His Word exactly what He planned for families. His instructions have not become outdated or irrelevant. They are designed to ensure a strong family unit that, in turn, creates a strong society. Unfortunately, we have seen an erosion of the family unit in the past few decades. As a result, we have seen changes in other areas of life. Psychologists have noted a correlation between the decline of the family and the decline of morality. There have been increases in crime, corruption, drug use, homelessness, and suicide.

What is happening? Why is the traditional concept of marriage and family being undermined? Lance Ponder offers a clear explanation of this process. He writes:

> Marriage and traditional family are under attack precisely because they are established by God. God created the institution of marriage in order to construct the best possible environment to raise healthy children. The homosexual movement strives to convince the general population that their behavior is acceptable, and they have a right to choose their sexual behavior. Once homosexual rights are established, the next step is to redefine marriage. By opening up marriages to relationships other than one man and one woman, marriage loses its value and ceases to have meaning. The only reason to redefine marriage is to destroy it. Men and

women are created with unique and special roles. The confusion of these roles is only to be expected when all standards erode in the chaos of relativism. The collapse of the family follows closely.[8]

Pope John Paul II summed it up saying, "As the family goes, so goes the nation and so goes the whole world in which we live."[9]

Let me close this chapter with a few ways the family is being challenged. Movies, television shows, and other forms of entertainment present alternative lifestyles and infidelity as acceptable and common. Pornography is more accessible to children and adults through online sites.

Many states have passed laws giving children the right to sue their parents. They can also receive birth control and get abortions without parental approval. School curricula are changing to include textbooks depicting alternative lifestyles, and "diversity and acceptance" are taught as values. And finally, LGBTQ groups advocate for the same marriage and family rights as traditional families, as well as promote gender-related policies that affect all areas of life.

It is important that we remain vigilant. First, as Christian families, we must live out our values and beliefs in our local communities. We must teach and train our children to follow God's principles. We must also advocate for policies and laws that support God's vision for marriage and family. Never forget that of all the issues facing our country, the state of the family has the most serious and long-term consequences. As such, we should give it our full attention, passionate involvement, and fervent prayers.

PROTECTION, MILITARY, AND FOREIGN POLICY

The world God created for Adam and Eve was perfect, without disease, hunger, or war. Man lived in harmony with God and His creation. Unfortunately, sin brought an end to this ideal environment and ushered in all forms of distress and dysfunction. Today, we live in a society of fear, distrust, and violence. America's peace is threatened by those within our borders as well as those from other countries. How does God expect us to handle these threats to our personal and national safety? Let's examine what His Word says about protection in general, as well as look at His perspective of the military and foreign policy.

Protection

Two of the primary issues of the 2022 midterm elections focused on safety within our country's borders and protection against foreign nations. The rise in violence in our cities, combined with a growing disrespect and lack of support for law enforcement, places individuals and businesses in vulnerable positions. Abroad, we see powerful countries positioning themselves to possibly bring harm to America. Each of these concerns highlights the importance of protection, both for the individual and for our nation. What does God have to say about our need for safety?

God as protector

God is known throughout the Bible as the Creator, Provider, and Almighty Lord. The Bible tells us He is omnipresent (always present), omniscient (all-knowing), and omnipotent (all powerful). As Christians, we should recognize that God is our ultimate Protector in times of trouble and against evil. The Psalms remind us of His power and protection:

> *Who is this King of glory? The Lord strong and mighty, The Lord mighty in battle* (Psalm 24:8).

> *He shields all who take refuge in him* (Psalm 18:30).

> *You are my hiding place; you will protect me from trouble and surround me with songs of deliverance* (Psalm 32:7).

> *You make your saving help my shield, and your right hand sustains me; your help has made me great. You provide a broad path for my feet, so that my ankles do not give way* (Psalm 18:35–36).

> *You are my refuge and my shield; I have put my hope in your word* (Psalm 119:114).

> *Lord, how many are my foes! How many rise up against me! . . . But you, Lord, are a shield around me, my glory, the One who lifts my head high* (Psalm 3:1, 3).

In the Old Testament, God promised physical protection to His people, the Israelites, when they kept the law (Deuteronomy 7:11–26). His divine protection kept them safe from the enemy nations they encountered as they entered the Promised Land. Exodus 23:27 says, *"I will send my terror ahead of you, and throw into confusion all the people among whom you come, and I will make all your enemies turn their backs to you."* God also provided His mighty protection to specific people who trusted in Him. He protected Daniel from the lions (Daniel 6:27), Shadrach, Meshach and Abed-nego from the fiery furnace (Daniel 3:38), Peter from imprisonment (Acts 12:1-11), and Paul from a variety of dangers, including shipwreck and a viper attack (Acts 27, 28). The same God who protected these individuals can and will protect us if we are willing to trust Him.

Protection at home

While we recognize God's providential protection, there are things that we can and should do to promote peace and safety in our country and throughout the world. Let's look first at our safety at home. First responders, such as police officers and firefighters, provide a first line of safety in our communities. Many communities have organized Crime Watch groups, where residents remain alert to what is happening in their neighborhood and notify law enforcement when they suspect trouble. The National Guard, the Coast Guard, and Border Patrol offer a nationwide second line of safety. While the Bible does not specifically address these positions of security, it does speak to peacekeepers and those in authority. Jesus said, *"Blessed are the peacemakers, for they will be called children of God"* (Matthew 5:9). Paul wrote to the Romans, *"Let every person be subject to the governing authorities for there is no authority except from God. The authorities that exist have been established by God"* (Romans 13:1-2).

Protection from outside danger

History is filled with accounts of aggression by one country towards another. These attacks are carried out for a variety of reasons. Most of these reasons can be summed up as being due to greed (wanting more land, resources, or power) or hate (racial, religious, or past relations). For nations desiring peace, protection from invasion is a priority. One of the ways we have seen nations protect their citizens is by erecting walls around their country. China began building a protective wall in the 7th Century BC. This Great Wall of China took more than 2000 years to construct. It is nearly 5500 miles long and is between 16 and 23 feet high.[1] Constructed around 650-600 BC, ancient Babylon's walls are over 300 feet high.[2] But even before these magnificent walls were built, God led Solomon to erect a wall around Jerusalem, the site of Israelites' temple (1 Kings 3:1). This wall measured 39 feet high and was nearly 8 feet thick. It was this same wall the Babylonians destroyed and Nehemiah and a remnant of Jews later rebuilt by (see the book of Nehemiah).

Today, countries still use walls as borders to protect citizens from outside attack. With the development of missiles, drones, and aircraft, walls may not offer the degree of protection as in the days of Babylon and Jerusalem, but they continue to provide a way to monitor who is entering a country and to serve as a barrier against many who would threaten our nation.

Military protection

America boasts of the finest military in the world. Thousands of men and women devote their lives to ensuring our safety. Through the efforts of our US Army, Navy, Marine Corp, Coast Guard, Air Force and now the US Space Force (as of 2019), we are protected from enemy attack. Our military also serve as peacekeepers across the world, working to protect others from harm. Unfortunately, these brave combatants may also be called to serve in wartime. What does God's word say about those who serve and about the concept of war?

Combatants

We have looked at the protection afforded our country through civil means, including law enforcement, citizen efforts, and barriers. These protections work well when the threat is from individuals or small groups of people, however, when the threat arises from another nation, a more organized and weaponized system of protection is required. This is where our military assumes responsibility.

Collectively, the men and women serving in our armed forces offer a level of defense that law enforcement and lay people cannot provide.

The Bible contains many references to soldiers. In the Old Testament, God used soldiers to protect His people. Saul established a permanent military (1 Samuel 13:2, 24:2, 26:2), while King David established a system of rotating troops with twelve groups of 24,000 men, each serving one month of the year (1 Chronicles 27). Here are a few more verses related to battle:

You armed me with strength for battle; You humbled my adversaries before me (Psalm 18:34).

For you have encircled me with strength for battle; You have forced those who rose up against me to bow down under me (Psalm 18:39).

A Psalm of David.
Blessed be the Lord, my rock,
Who trains my hands for war,
And my fingers for battle;
My lovingkindness and my fortress,
My stronghold and my deliverer,
My shield and he in whom I take refuge,
Who subdues my people under me (Psalm 144:1-2).

In the New Testament, we see Jesus' interaction with a Roman Centurion (an officer in charge of one hundred soldiers). Jesus did not denounce his role as an officer. Instead, He praised the soldier's faith and understanding of authority (Matthew 8:5-13).[3] The apostle Paul often used military references when teaching the new believers. In 2 Timothy 2:4, he wrote, *"No one serving as a soldier gets entangled in civilian affairs, but rather tries to please his commanding officer."* He describes his friend, Epaphroditus, as a *"fellow soldier"* (Philippians 2:25) and used the analogy of battle armor to describe how a Christian is to be *"strong in the Lord"* (Ephesians 6:10-20).

War

A discussion of the military would not be complete without looking at the concept and reality of war. Ecclesiastes 3:8 reminds us that there is *"a time to love and a time to hate; A time for war and a time for peace."* As noted earlier, the Old Testament describes many instances where God led His people into battle. For example, we read in Deuteronomy 20, *"When you go to war against your enemies and see horses and chariots and an army greater than yours, do not be afraid of them... Do not be fainthearted or afraid; do not panic or be terrified by them. For the Lord your God is the one who goes with you to fight for you against your enemies to give you victory"* (vs 1-4). Joshua, David, and Gideon led the Israelites into battle and in most cases, these battles were both destructive and deadly.

One of the most compelling stories in the life of Abraham is recorded in Genesis 14. His nephew, Lot, was residing in the Jordan Valley near Sodom. While there, four enemy kings invaded the land, taking Lot and his family captive. When Abraham learned that his nephew had been captured, he immediately set out on a rescue mission with what is probably the first recorded army – 318 trained men from his own family. In the very next chapter, we hear what God thought about Abraham's actions: *"After these things, the word of the Lord came to Abram in a vision, saying, 'Do not fear, Abram, I am a shield to you; Your reward shall be very great'"* (Genesis 15:1[NASB]).

As a young boy, David fought Goliath because the large Philistine was taunting the army of Israel, intending to take them as slaves. David's final words to Goliath clearly stated his purpose in fighting. He said, *"This day the Lord will deliver you up into my hands...that all the earth may know that there is a God in Israel...for the battle is the Lord's"* (1 Samuel 17: 46-47[NASB]).

Those who oppose the concept of war draw upon the fact that there are no instances of battle recorded in the New Testament. Instead, we hear Jesus teaching us to *"turn the other cheek"* and to pray for our enemies (Matthew 5:38-44). Yet later, in John 15:13, Jesus tells us that *"greater love has no man than this, that a man lay down his life for his friends"* (RSV). How do we reconcile these verses? Are they contradictory? Or can we identify an underlying principle that recognizes both perspectives? I believe that God looks more at our hearts and attitudes than our actions. He is more concerned about the "why" behind our actions. If we wage war for personal gain, power, or pride, we are operating from a selfish position that is not God-honoring. However, as in the cases of Abraham and David, if evil people or nations seek to harm others, we demonstrate selflessness when we wage war to protect innocent people. For example, in the early 1930's, Adolf Hitler and the Nazi forces set out to establish supremacy for the Germanic people to rule and dominate the earth. This led to the oppression and death of thousands of Jews and the start of World War II in 1939. But God brought together many nations to act as allies to defeat this evil cause.[4]

Foreign Policy

How should America approach other countries? Over the years, we have seen foreign policy range from isolationism, to neutrality, to engagement in world conflict. We have heard Theodore Roosevelt say, "Speak softly and carry a big stick." In June 1987, President Reagan challenged the Soviet General Secretary, Mikhail Gorbachev in front of the Berlin wall with the words, "Mr. Gorbachev, open this gate! Mr. Gorbachev, tear down this wall!" Those words mark the end of forty years of the Cold War. And following the attacks on September 11, 2001, George W. Bush sounded this warning, "All nations should know: America will do what is necessary to ensure our nation's security."[5] International organizations such as the United Nations and the North Atlantic Treaty Organization (NATO) bring nations together as allies and advocates for peace. As Christians, we recognize the seriousness of foreign policy, but what is God's perspective on this topic? Does the Bible give us any guidance for America?

While the Bible provides general guidelines for how we are to relate with others, it does not address specific issues. Bryan Chapell, clerk of the Presbyterian Church in America, noted, "Scripture is not telling us specific foreign policies or alliances our nation is to support or oppose in contemporary times; but, Scripture is giving us the standards of justice, righteousness, integrity, generosity and sound governance that should direct our leaders' decisions and actions both domestically and internationally."[6]

In a survey of evangelical leaders, 94% said that the Bible significantly or somewhat influences their personal views on US foreign policy and alliances. Many of these leaders noted that they don't believe the Bible gives specific instructions regarding policies with foreign countries but does offer principles of engagement. It is precisely for this reason that we need to have a firm understanding of the principles taught in the Bible. The same principles that we have discussed in regard to relationships, wealth, loyalty, and leadership should also guide our policies with other nations. Even when Scripture doesn't speak to a particular situation or circumstance, we must consider the character of God and seek His leading. There was a popular phrase many years ago that was known by the letters WWJD ("What would Jesus do?"). The answers provided in the Bible will help us clarify "What should America do?"

SOCIAL ISSUES

Americans come in all shapes, sizes, races, cultures, and experiences. Each person is unique, with his or her individual needs and desires. When faced with the possibility that these needs and desires will not be met, that individual has the option to give up or speak up. Today, we face many issues about which people differ in their opinion of what is right. Race, immigration, healthcare, and education are some of the most widely discussed topics. It seems nearly unimaginable to think that we as a nation could ever reach agreement on these important topics, but we are challenged as Christians to live in harmony with everyone (Romans 12:18). How is this possible? I believe that most of the social issues our country faces could be addressed by two well-known phrases: *"Love your neighbor as yourself"* (Matthew 22:39) and "Walk a mile in my shoes," originally suggested in a poem by Mary Lathrap in 1895. Let's see how we can apply these ideas to a few social concerns.

Race and Racism

The concepts of race and racism are found throughout the Bible. Genesis 1:27 states, *"God created mankind in his own image."* We do not know whether that refers only to man's character and soul or whether it also refers to man's physical appearance. In either situation, race is not mentioned. Caleb Mathis, in an article entitled *What Does the Bible Say About Race?* wrote:

In the creation story, what the Bible doesn't mention is just as important as the few details it does give. The Bible makes no mention of the race or ethnicity of the first couple—probably because that wasn't the point. The main message was that humanity, every single person who has lived and died on planet Earth, was created in God's image. The color of one's skin, or the ethnic heritage of one's ancestors, didn't actually factor into the equation. There is a weight and worth to human life—of all colors, shades, and backgrounds—that exceeds the rest of creation. To fall in line with this value is to fall in line with God's original intent for this planet.[1]

After the flood, the Bible says that the sons of Noah moved into the surrounding areas to raise their families. Later, in Genesis 11, we read that people began building a tower at Babel to show their skills and power. God was displeased that the people were not recognizing His provision, so He *"confused their language."* This resulted in groups of people moving to various regions. Again, the focus was on location and language rather than race. During ancient times, people did not travel large distances. Most people lived and died within a ten-mile radius of where they were born. Therefore, the concept of people living in unfamiliar places may have caused fear, prejudice, and even hatred, but these feelings were generally centered on national or tribal association rather than race. Throughout the Old Testament, the Israelite nation encountered hostility from other nations, but again, this hostility was either related to defense of their land or from differences in the gods these nations worshiped.

In the New Testament, Jesus did not treat people differently because of race. His teachings highlighted the fact that every person, regardless of race, language, or reputation, is loved by God and can become a follower of Jesus. His great commission was to go into all the world and preach the gospel to every nation (Matthew 28:18-20). He later provided details about this command, saying, *"But you will receive power when the Holy Spirit comes on you; and you will be my witnesses in Jerusalem, and in all Judea and Samaria, and to the ends of the earth"* (Acts 1:8).

During the time Jesus lived, people from Samaria were looked down on by Jews, but we see Jesus striking up a conversation with a Samaritan woman (John 4). In one of Jesus' parables, the hero of the story is a Samaritan. In Acts 8, we read that Philip was sent to share the gospel in Samaria. He was later led by an angel to an encounter with an Egyptian eunuch, who heard the Gospel, accepted it, and was baptized. The apostle Paul wrote, *"Here there is no Gentile or Jew, circumcised or uncircumcised, barbarian, Scythian, slave or free, but Christ is all, and is in all"* (Colossians 3:11). Finally, in Revelation, we see the saints gathered around the throne, praising Jesus, singing, *"You are worthy to take the scroll and to open its seals, because you were slain, and with your blood you purchased for God persons from every tribe and language and people and nation. You have made them to be a kingdom and priests to serve our God"* (Revelation 5:9-10).

Prejudice against people based on where they lived was very evident throughout Scripture. Even the religious leaders exhibited prejudice against Gentiles, refusing to eat with them and avoiding travel through their towns. Today, we base our opinions of others primarily upon differences in skin tone. American racism makes assumptions about everything — intentions, lifestyle choices, mental capacities, and beyond — from external appearances of color.[2] It is clear, though, that the Bible does not consider one race to be superior to another. Jesus did not see race. Racism is man's prejudice. Malachi 2:10 reads, *"Do we not all have one Father? Did not one God create us? Why do we profane the covenant of our ancestors by being unfaithful to one another?"*

While most Christians would say that they are not racist, Timothy Keller highlights another response that we should consider, writing:

> There is always a danger of putting so much emphasis on the unity of the human race that we come to insist that race is unimportant as the older liberalism taught, namely that we should be completely 'color-blind.' But it is also possible, especially today in the time of the newer progressivism and

identity politics, to put too much emphasis on irreconcilable diversity, so no racial group has the right to "speak into" the experience of the other, which obscures our common humanity."[3]

Christians are called to face the problem of racism and we have been provided unique tools to use. Todd Wilson writes that Christians realize God expects us to be personally responsible for how we relate with all people, regardless of race. We also recognize that every human being is made in the image of God and is thus of equal worth and dignity. Additionally, Christians know the relationships can be transformed when we get to know others on a personal level. Finally, through our own experience we know the possibility of genuine heart renewal through faith in Jesus.[4]

We must take care that we do not isolate specific verses that support ungodly attitudes. Mathis summarizes the attitudes we must be willing to adopt in our own lives and dealings with others. He writes, "Cherry-picking a verse here or a story there, you may be able to paint a misguided image of God or his people. But when you wrestle with the full extent of scripture, you find a God of creativity, who crafted people of all shapes, sizes, and colors, calling them very good. And when those people ran away from them, he chased them down. He is a God of diversity, love, and freedom."[5]

Immigration

Related closely to the problem of racism is the topic of immigration. This is especially significant today as thousands of illegal immigrants are entering our country through its southern border. America has always been a country that accepted people from other nations who were being persecuted or who lacked basic needs. We have provided a process for citizenship to anyone truly desiring to come and be a productive member of our society. Yet God's Word calls us to be discerning, recognizing that there are others coming into our country who do not have good intentions. As mentioned in an earlier chapter, the city of Jerusalem had walls to protect its citizens against those who would seek to harm them. We should also have a system in place to screen those entering our country.

You will not find the terms "immigrant" or "refugee" in the Bible. Instead, those who leave one place for another are referred to as "sojourners" or "foreigners." The Bible gives specific instructions for how these people are to be treated. First, we are called to love our neighbor as ourselves (Leviticus 19:18). The Israelites were commanded, *"Do not mistreat foreigners who are living in your land. Treat them as you would an Israelite and love them as you love yourselves. Remember that you were once foreigners in the land of Egypt. I am the Lord your God"* (Leviticus 19:33-34[GNT]).

For example, the book of Ruth is about a widow from the tribe of Moab who chooses to accompany her mother-in-law, Naomi, back to Israel and live there with her. Boaz demonstrated kindness and compassion towards Ruth as she gathered grain from his field and later offered the protection of marriage to the young widow. Ruth and Boaz were the parents of Obed, who was the grandfather of King David.

As mentioned earlier, most people living in ancient times did not travel far from home, so their understanding of "neighbor" was someone living within their town, but as I said earlier, Jesus, in His parable of the good Samaritan, expanded the scope of neighbors to those from other regions or countries (Luke 10: 29-37). We are to meet their physical needs, respect their dignity with compassion, and protect them from abuse. The apostle Paul wrote, *"Let no one seek his own good, but the good of his neighbor"* (1 Corinthians 10:24). Jesus challenged his listeners, saying:

> *You have heard that it was said, 'Love your neighbor, and hate your enemy.' But I tell you, love your enemies and pray for those who persecute you, that you may be children of your Father in heaven. He causes his sun to rise on the evil and the good, and sends rain on the righteous and*

the unrighteous. If you love those who love you, what reward will you get?
Are not even the tax collectors doing that? And if you greet only your
own people, what are you doing more than others? Do not even pagans
do that?" (Matthew 5:43-48)

The apostle Paul encouraged a similar response in Titus 3:14, saying, *"Our people must learn to devote themselves to doing what is good, in order to provide for urgent needs and not live unproductive lives."* The Samaritan in Jesus' parable fulfilled these requirements by showing compassion to the beaten man despite dangerous conditions and by paying for the man's care from his own resources without expectation of repayment.[6]

Another aspect of immigration frequently overlooked is that many immigrants who come to America are already Christians. They come to the US from other Christian nations, such as Brazil, Mexico, and the Philippines.[7] Many are fleeing persecution for their Christian faith. Additionally, significant numbers of people are coming from countries where Christianity is illegal. For example, Islamic countries often view other religions as heretical, an affront to Allah, which is considered an extremely serious crime. Communist countries, by comparison, often outlaw all religion.[8] There is a strong likelihood that these refugees have never been exposed to the gospel of Jesus, hence, immigration provides an opportunity for sharing the gospel with them. The apostle Paul explained that God orchestrates the times and movements of people saying, *"He did this so that they might seek God, and perhaps they might reach out and find him…"* (Acts 17:27 [HCSB]). Is it possible that God has a missionary purpose in migration and that we are missing that perspective?[9]

In today's political climate, many are fearful of how the growing numbers of immigrants will impact our country. As Christians, we must view each fear and opinion in light of Scripture and accurate information. We must not have knee-jerk reactions, condemning all immigration and refusing to meet the needs of those who are here. Alternately, we should not blindly accept everyone without consideration of their intentions toward our country. As we consider how to approach those who are "foreigners," let's remember that we as Christians are also sojourners. The apostle Paul tells us that we are *"no longer foreigners and strangers, but fellow citizens with God's people"* (Ephesians 2:19). We are here on a temporary journey, with heaven as our final home (Hebrews 11:13-16). We need to also remember that God is ultimately in control of all circumstances. He calls us to bring the issue of immigration before His throne. Let's pray, asking God to:

1. Protect America from all who seek to harm us.
2. Give our leaders discernment and guidance in establishing policies to address the needs of people throughout the world, as well as establishing and implementing national policies of immigration.
3. Provide the necessary resources to meet the overwhelming needs of those who come to the United States.
4. Provide opportunities for sharing the gospel of Christ.

Finally, we as Christians must be willing to take an active role in this issue. The eyes of the world watch to see how we respond to those in need. We have the high calling to demonstrate Christ's love towards those we come in contact with, being salt and light to those who need Him.

Healthcare

As a social issue, healthcare relates to everyone living in the United States. Recent events surrounding COVID-19 have demonstrated the vulnerability we all face regarding our personal health. Most people quickly agree that preventative medicine is vital to maintaining optimal health, but beyond that, opinions vary. Let's look at what the Bible says about health and caring for the sick.

One of my favorite names for God is found in Exodus 17:15. "Jehovah Rapha" means "The Lord Who Heals You." This refers not only to physical healing, but also mental, emotional, and spiritual healing. As someone with a chronic disease, knowing that God identifies Himself as the Healer is especially meaningful. Jesus is also described as the Great Physician based on His comments in Luke 4:23 and Luke 5:31-32. Numerous verses related to health and healing are found throughout the Bible. Here are a few to consider:

I will take away sickness from among you, and none will miscarry or be barren in your land. I will give you a full life span (Exodus 23:25-26).

Lord my God, I called to you for help, and you healed me (Psalm 30:2).

I will bind up the injured, and I will strengthen the weak (Ezekiel 34:16).

Heal the sick, raise the dead, cleanse those who have leprosy,[a] drive out demons. Freely you have received; freely give (Matthew 10:8).

Is anyone among you sick? Let them call the elders of the church to pray over them and anoint them with oil in the name of the Lord (James 5:14).

Dear friend, I pray that you may enjoy good health and that all may go well with you (3 John 1:2).

The Bible encourages us to take care of our bodies first because He created us and, secondly, for believers, our bodies are temples for the Holy Spirit (1 Corinthians 6:19-20). God's Word also offers a few suggestions for how to promote healing. For example, bandaging wounds (Isaiah 1:6), using oil and wine as topical agents (James 5:14; Luke 10:34), and using wine for stomach problems (1 Timothy 5:23) are presented as "holistic" treatments. Drugs and other forms of treatment are not mentioned, as they had not been invented at the time the Bible was written. However, that does not mean that Christians should not take advantage of all medical options available to treat health concerns.

Jesus provides the best example of healing in the Bible. He healed people everywhere He went and did not make distinction between rich and poor, young and old, or Jew and Gentile. He healed everyone who came to Him. Jesus also demonstrated a variety of healing "techniques," including touch (Matthew 8:15; Luke 13:13) and speaking a healing command (Matthew 9:6-7). He used clay (John 9:6) and His own saliva (Mark 8:22-25) to heal the blind. Some were healed simply by touching His clothing (Matthew 9:20-22; Matthew 14:35-36). In fact, on several occasions, Jesus healed people who were not physically present (Matthew 8:13; Matthew 15:28; John 4:50-53). It is clear that Jesus has the power and the desire to heal all types of illness and infirmity. After His death and resurrection, He gave the disciples the ability to heal through the power of the Holy Spirit. The book of Acts records the healing of the lame, diseased, and those afflicted with unclean spirits (3:1-8; 5:15-16).

Mark Coppenger, in his article, *The Bible and Health Care*, highlights a few other truths related to health and health care.[10] He notes that doctoring is biblical. In addition to Jesus, Luke (the author of the gospel bearing his name) was a physician. God has also provided medical resources in nature, including herbs for digestion, willow bark used to make aspirin, and mold used to make penicillin. Coppenger notes that the primary responsibility for health and health care lies with the individual and the family. The apostle Paul wrote to families, saying, *"Anyone who does not provide for their relatives, and especially for their own household, has denied the faith and is worse than an unbeliever"* (1 Timothy 5:8).

Now that we have recognized health and healing are biblical, what does the Bible say about how healthcare should be provided? Is healthcare a right or a privilege? Is it the responsibility of individual medical practitioners or the government? And what role do charitable organizations such as faith-based hospitals and secular organizations such as the Red Cross and United Way play in meeting healthcare needs? The answers to these questions are not simple. Many people believe that access to quality healthcare is a fundamental right of all

Americans. They continue the argument to conclude that the government should manage healthcare for all people. Those who oppose this believe that healthcare, while important, should be viewed as a privilege and managed by the actual medical practitioners in cooperation with the patient and his/her family.

First, let's consider whether healthcare is a "right" for all citizens. Neil Mammon, in his book *40 Days Towards a More Godly Nation*, provides a way to distinguish "rights" from "good" (i.e. "privilege"). He writes, "Many people confuse 'rights' with 'goods.' It's critical to differentiate the two. Here's an easy way to look at it: If a 'right' depends on someone else's service, work, or money, it's not a right, it's goods, and it's certainly not a God given or Constitutional Right." [11]

Based on this definition, healthcare would be a "good/ service" that is contingent on someone else providing the service. When we begin guaranteeing services to people who require other people to do the work, we are being presumptuous and forcing a person to meet someone else's needs. That said, I also believe that the Bible calls Christians to do more to ensure quality healthcare for those in need. We must be wise and discerning, both individually (in how we take care of our personal health) and as a nation (in how we provide healthcare to the masses). God's word tells us that He *"will supply all our needs according to his glorious riches in Christ Jesus"* (Philippians 4:19 CSB).

Education

Let's now turn our attention to a third and key area that impacts many Americans, especially those with children. Having been raised by educators, I decided as a young child that I wanted to be a teacher, as well. Education was important to my parents and they wanted their children to have the best education possible. I believe this has been true for most people for generations. People who have grown up with little in the way of material things look at education as a way to get a better paying job, thus making it possible to have a better way of life.

For some, education equates with wealth, power, security, and status. So what priority should education have in our lives? Who is responsible for ensuring a strong education for today's youth? Finally, what should we be teaching in our schools? The Bible, while it doesn't speak to the public school system that we have put in place in America, has much to say about learning.

Knowledge, understanding, and wisdom

Before we look at what the Bible has to say about education, we need to look at a few words that seem to be intertwined throughout Scripture. The terms knowledge, wisdom, and understanding are often used together in verses. For example, Proverbs 2:10-11 reads, *"For wisdom will enter your heart, and knowledge will be pleasant to your soul. Discretion will protect you, and understanding will guard you."* I like to look at these terms as a progression of learning. First, knowledge is acquired. We may get knowledge from many sources, including books, teachers, and experiences. Once we have the information (knowledge), we move to understanding. Ask anyone who has taken English Literature in school; it's one thing to know the characters and plot (knowledge), but comprehension (understanding) is much more challenging. Understanding implies mastery of the topic and may require time to practice the concepts.

For many people, learning stops at this point, but Christians are expected to take education one step further. We are to combine our knowledge with wisdom. Wisdom has been defined as rightly applying knowledge. We cannot learn wisdom on our own, for God is the source of wisdom, however, the Bible tells us that if we lack wisdom, we *"should ask God, who gives generously to all without finding fault, and it will be given to you"* (James 1:5, 6). Without godly wisdom, we run the risk of becoming proud in our knowledge, puffed up, and arrogant. So now, let's look at a few verses related to learning:

Instruct the wise and they will be wiser still; teach the righteous and they will add to their learning (Proverbs 9:9).

Whoever gives heed to instruction prospers, and blessed is the one who trusts in the Lord (Proverbs 16:20).

The heart of the discerning acquires knowledge, for the ears of the wise seek it out (Proverbs 18:15).

To these four young men God gave knowledge and understanding of all kinds of literature and learning (Daniel 1:17).

My people are destroyed from lack of knowledge (Hosea 4:6).

Until I come, devote yourself to the public reading of Scripture, to preaching and to teaching (1 Timothy 4:13).

Do your best to present yourself to God as one approved, a worker who does not need to be ashamed and who correctly handles the word of truth (2 Timothy 2:15).

For this very reason, make every effort to add to your faith goodness; and to goodness, knowledge... (2 Peter 1:5.)

Biblical examples

The Bible provides several examples of men who were well-educated and whom God used to accomplish great things. Moses was raised as the son of the Egyptian Pharaoh's daughter. Acts 7:22 tells us that *"Moses was educated in all the learning of the Egyptians, and was powerful in speech and action."* In Egypt, students were taught reading, writing, mathematics, medicine, geography, history, music, and science. The *Book of Instruction* was used to teach morality, ethics, and humanities. Since Moses was in the royal household, he would have received a specialized education that was reserved for children of the nobility. This included instruction on the ways of court and religious teaching. Many of the children of noble households would leave their education to become priests and scribes.[12]

It is widely accepted that King Solomon was one of the wisest men to ever live. 1 Kings 4:29-30 states, *"God gave Solomon wisdom and very great insight, and a breadth of understanding as measureless as the sand on the seashore. Solomon's wisdom was greater than the wisdom of all the people of the East, and greater than all the wisdom of Egypt."* The passage goes on to say that he wrote three thousand proverbs and more than a thousand songs. He was knowledgeable about a wide variety of animals and plants. People from all over the world came to listen to Solomon's wisdom.

As a young man, Daniel was taken captive by the Babylonians and was appointed to serve in the king's service. Daniel 1:4 notes that the king was looking for *"young men without any physical defect, handsome, showing aptitude for every kind of learning, well informed, quick to understand, and qualified to serve in the king's palace."* Daniel would be taught the language and literature of the Babylonians.

In the New Testament, we meet Paul (formerly Saul), a Roman by birth and a devout Jew. He had been educated by Gamaliel, one of the most influential teachers of that day (Acts 22:3). Paul was not only knowledgeable about Jewish beliefs and culture, but he was also well-versed in the beliefs, religions, and cultures of others. He was able to reason with the Stoic and Epicurean philosophers and to make a strong case for Jesus before the religious and political leaders of his day.

We should also note that God does not look down on the unlearned. There is no evidence in the Bible that Jesus was educated beyond the knowledge and skills he received at home. Additionally, many of Jesus' followers were skilled laborers with little to no education. While education is important, it is not mandatory in order to be a follower of Christ.

Who should teach?

First, the Bible gives parents the ultimate responsibility to oversee their child's education. As described in a previous chapter, parents are instructed to *"train up a child in the way he should go"* (Proverbs 22:6 [RSV]). Fathers are also admonished to *"bring them* (their children) *up in the training and instruction of the Lord"* (Ephesians 6:4). The Bible also allows for others to provide instruction (Ephesians 4:11,12), but calls on these teachers to be wise. Those who would presume to teach must do so with wisdom and integrity, for Scripture says they will be judged more strictly than others (James 3:1). I believe this to be true because teachers have great influence in their students' lives. They have the ability to guide their thoughts and attitudes about themselves and the world around them. They have the ability to inspire or destroy. Jesus, in speaking of children and new believers, said, *"Whoever causes one of these little ones who believe in me to stumble, it would be better for him to have a heavy millstone hung around his neck, and to be drowned in the depth of the sea"* (Matthew 18:6). These sound like harsh words, but they indicate the high standards and expectations God places on those who teach.

What should we be teaching?

First, we should be teaching Scripture. This is the foundation for all learning, providing wisdom and discernment. Through Scripture, God is able to instruct and teach the way we are to go (Psalm 32:8). The psalmist wrote,

> *Open my eyes that I may see wonderful things in your law.*
> *I am a stranger on earth; do not hide your commands from me.*
> *My soul is consumed with longing for your laws at all times.*
> *You rebuke the arrogant, who are accursed, those who stray from your commands.*
> *Remove from me their scorn and contempt, for I keep your statutes.*
> *Though rulers sit together and slander me, your servant will meditate on your decrees.*
> *Your statutes are my delight; they are my counselors*
> (Psalm 119:18-24).

Second, we should learn things necessary for caring for the world God has given us. He gave Adam the responsibility of overseeing everything in the Garden of Eden. We still carry that responsibility today. While God does not need us to care for His creation (He is perfectly capable of that Himself), He allows us the privilege of serving Him in this way. Subjects such as biology, botany, agriculture, and math provide knowledge to care for man, the animals, and plant life. Other sciences – chemistry, physics, and even meteorology – aid our understanding of how we can employ the materials God has provided to create a better way of life for man.

The Bible also calls us to have a knowledge of history. Throughout the Old Testament, the people of Israel retold the stories of how God had cared for them by rescuing them from slavery and bringing them to the Promised Land. These stories were passed down from one generation to the next so they would not only remember what had taken place, but also would learn from the past. In the New Testament, Paul often reminded his listeners about past events to establish the foundation of his message that Jesus was the Messiah prophesied years before (Acts 13:16-41). History as a subject can give us insight into the lives of those who lived before us, as well as provide guidance about what we should and should not do in the future.

Finally, knowledge of literature and the arts is described in Scripture. While not necessary for daily life, an appreciation for literature, art, and music uplifts the soul and provides a means of expression that isn't found in other areas of life. Music is used throughout Scripture as a means of praise and worship. Miriam, Aaron's sister and the sister of Moses, led the Israelites in worship with a tambourine and dancing (Exodus 15:20). King David was also seen dancing to celebrate the return of the Ark of the Covenant to Jerusalem (2 Samuel 6:14), and we read that Paul and Silas sang hymns of praise in jail (Acts 16:25).

As mentioned in the previous section, education should be considered a privilege rather than a right. As with healthcare, education should be made available through a variety of options. Public, private, and charter schools provide learning opportunities for millions of American children. Many families choose to take responsibility for their children's education through homeschooling. No one option is right for every family, but I believe the Bible clearly tells us that the final decision about what their child will learn and where that learning will take place lies with parents. Let us remember that Paul encourages us to do everything (including learning) for the glory of God (1 Corinthians 10:13).

PART 3 Introduction

We have looked at the history of our country and learned what God's Word says about many of the issues we currently face. Now it's time to put our knowledge to work. It is time to live out our faith in our homes, communities, and abroad. In the following chapters, we will establish a better understanding of who we are as Christians and how we can develop a strong, effective witness. We will also learn how God can multiply our efforts as we join with other Christians to impact the world for Him. Let's get started!

PREPARE TO STAND - ESTABLISH A FIRM FOUNDATION

O ne of my greatest joys is being able to say with absolute certainty that I am a Christian. The first mention of the term "Christian" is found in Acts 11:26 and referred to the early disciples in Antioch. Later, King Agrippa recognized the apostle Paul as being a Christian, implying a negative connotation of someone who follows Jesus (Acts 26:27-30). In truth, a study of history reveals many atrocities committed by people claiming to be Christians, although their actions clearly indicate that they were not followers of Christ based on what the Bible teaches. So what about us? What does it mean to be a Christian? What makes us different from those who do not know Jesus as Savior? What gives us the strength to stand for God in today's world?

Our Identity as Christians

Christians are people who have a personal relationship with God through his Son, Jesus. We recognize that God has a plan for us and we seek to live out that purpose. The Bible also assigns us unique titles, or identities, that describe our role in society.

Chosen People

Our first identification clearly sets us apart from those who do not follow Jesus. 1 Peter 2:9 reminds us that we *are a chosen people, a royal priesthood, a holy nation, God's special possession, that you may declare the praises of him who called you out of darkness into his wonderful light.* Is there anything more wonderful than knowing that God has chosen you to be a part of His family? We all love being chosen – to be on the team, to be first in line, to be given the better job. How much more special is it to be chosen to be a child of God? Yet notice the last part of our verse – why we are chosen. God has chosen us so that we may praise Him. Being a part of God's family is not about us, it's about Him. Rick Warren, in his best-selling book, *The Purpose-Driven Life*, opens the very first chapter with this sentence: "It's not about you."[1] He adds that we were born for God's purpose.

The next two descriptions in our verse indicate the holiness of the life we are called to live. We are to be a royal priesthood and a holy nation, both of which imply living according to God's laws daily and maintaining a God-pleasing lifestyle. In order to follow His laws, we must know Him and His Word intimately. Have you recognized your standing with God? Do you realize that you are special, created by God for His pleasure and purpose? It is only after grasping this concept that we are ready to move to our next title.

Ambassadors

In 2 Corinthians, Paul refers to Christians as ambassadors for Christ, given the ministry of sharing the gospel with others (5:19-20). An ambassador is one who is authorized to represent or send a message on behalf of another person.[2] Christians are given the authority and responsibility to represent Jesus and to speak his message of salvation to a lost world. To refuse to do so could be considered a dereliction of duty. In Mark 16:15, Jesus tells his disciples to go into all the world and preach the gospel. Later, in Matthew 28:19, he gives the commandment, often referred to as the Great Commission, to "*go and make disciples of all nations.*" Greg Laurie writes that 95 percent of all Christians have never led another person to Christ.[3] He adds, "For many followers of Jesus, the Great Commission has instead become the Great Omission, and this is more than a pity; it's a travesty." We should view our mission of witnessing as a great calling and an exciting experience. We should be eager to tell others about the wonderful plan

God has for them. But are we? Consider this: Do we talk more about our football team, politics, or the latest movie than we do about Jesus? Are we more interested in our own pursuits than in faithfully serving our Lord by sharing His message with others?

Servants

Another title used to describe Christians is that of servant. Jesus said of Himself, *"the Son of Man did not come to be served, but to serve and give his life as a ransom for many"* (Matthew 20:28). His entire life was a picture of service. He took care of a wine shortage at a wedding (John 2:1-10), fed large groups of people (Luke 6:35-44; 8:1-9), healed the sick (Mark 1:29-34; 3:1-6), rescued distressed sailors (Matthew 8:23-26), and even washed dirty, dusty feet (John 13:1-20). He calls us to that same life. While many of the things Jesus did were miraculous, we can offer similar service to our own families and communities. Having a servant mentality is about attitude – seeking the good of others before ourselves. We will discuss what a servant lifestyle looks like in more detail later but let me encourage you to look around and see what you can be doing right now to serve others.

Salt and Light

Finally, we are called to be salt and light. In Matthew 5, Jesus taught that we are the salt of the earth and the light of the world (vs. 13-14). What exactly did He mean by these descriptions? Let's look first at salt. I don't know about you, but I often crave salty food. Salt is a natural mineral that is commonly found in all parts of the world. It is necessary to sustain life, but it also serves many useful purposes. First, it brings out the natural flavors of the food, thus enhancing its taste. Salt is also used to preserve food, fight weeds, and fertilize soil. Those who raise livestock know that animals require salt to maintain a healthy appetite and weight. Those of you who live in cold climates know salt melts snow and ice, making our roads and walkways safer. In applying these ideas to Christians, we first recognize the "commonness" or everyday usefulness of our lives. We have the ability to improve life for others, to whet their appetite for Christ, and to solve daily challenges, but Jesus also gives us a warning. He says, *"But if the salt loses its saltiness, how can it be made salty again? It is no longer good for anything, except to be thrown out and trampled underfoot"* (vs 13).

The second metaphor Jesus uses in this passage is the idea that we are to be light. Bright, sunny days bring happiness and joy to children and adults alike. Things always take on a more positive perspective in the light of day. Light serves to dispel darkness, allowing us to see the dangers, and obstacles around us. It allows us to see clearly where we are going. As Christians, we are challenged to bring the positive perspective of Christ to others and to expose the sin and obstacles that prevent people from living the life God's desires for them. Jesus describes us as a light in a city or a lamp on a table, lighting the area for ourselves and others.

Picture a crowd of people wandering lost in the dark. One person has a large flashlight that could help others see, but instead, he chooses to go home without offering help. We would call that person selfish and uncaring. How much more seriously should we take our responsibility to be Christ's light for those who do not know Him? Jesus concluded this passage, saying *"let your light shine before others, that they may see your good deeds and glorify your Father in heaven"* (Matthew 5:16).

Becoming a Child of God

What about you? Have you recognized the truth about Jesus and accepted the salvation and eternal life with Him that He offers? Perhaps you have been a Christian for a while but have never made a total commitment to live out your faith. Some of you may have fears about how being a Christian will affect your everyday lifestyle. I challenge you to develop a radical faith that will motivate you to make changes, take risks, and give everything you have to serving Christ.

I want to speak for just a moment to the man or woman reading this who recognizes deep within that they do not know Jesus as Savior and have not received His joy. Allow me to share how you can make this life-changing decision:

First, recognize your current situation. The Bible says that we are all sinners and fall short of God's expectations (Romans 3:23). God is righteous and holy, and our sin keeps us from having a relationship with Him. There is nothing we can do to change that by ourselves. No amount of being good or doing good can make us clean in His sight. And the consequence of our sin is death (Romans 6:23). Therefore, we need a Savior.

Second, believe that Jesus is the only way that we can be forgiven and found acceptable to God. When Jesus died on the cross, He paid the penalty for every sin that you and I have or will commit. John 3:16 tells us, *"God so loved the world that he gave his one and only Son, that whoever believes in him shall not perish but have eternal life."* I love the little word "so" in this verse. God doesn't just love us, He loves us *so much*. Why would we not want to receive that love through Christ? This verse also tells us that this gift of salvation is for everyone, no matter who they are or what they have done in the past. No one is "too bad" for God's forgiveness. Likewise, no one is "too good" to not need that same forgiveness.

Finally, confess Jesus as your Lord and Savior. The Bible says that if we believe in our hearts and confess it with our mouths, we will be saved (Romans 10:9). Period. Done deal. You may not hear angels sing or feel a rush of power, but this simple act has eternal consequences. You immediately receive the Holy Spirit and become a child of the King. Welcome to the family of God!

The Power of Prayer

As we prepare to live for God, it is vital that we develop an intimate relationship with Him. The primary way to do this is through prayer.

Besides just reciting memorized prayers or saying a daily blessing at mealtime, I'm talking about personal, honest, genuine prayers when you talk to God and allow Him to talk to you. Jeremiah 29:12-13 promises that when we pray, He will hear us. God tells us, *"You will seek me and find me when you seek me with all your heart."* 2 Chronicles 7:14 encourages us to pray for our nation, saying *"if my people, who are called by my name, will humble themselves and pray and seek my face and turn from their wicked ways, then I will hear from heaven, and I will forgive their sin and will heal their land."*

There are many books and Bible studies written on the importance of prayer and providing suggestions for establishing a strong prayer life. I would like to mention just a few of those suggestions:

Consistent prayer

Pray consistently. It doesn't matter if it is first thing in the morning, before you go to sleep, or sometime during the day. Consider it an appointment with God. Schedule time in your day to be in God's presence. The Bible tells us that we should pray continuously, without ceasing (1 Thessalonians 5:17). Develop a lifestyle of prayer. Set out reminders to pray. And then pray. Get to know the God who loves you.

Specific prayer

God wants us to pray for specific needs. Some may say that He should already know what we need or want, but He still wants us to ask. Jesus told His disciples, *"Until now you have not asked for anything in my name. Ask and you will receive, and your joy will be complete"* (John 16:24). One of the benefits of specific prayer is that you will recognize when God answers. Over the years, I have prayed many specific requests. Many times, I prayed for something I needed. Other times, it was for wisdom to make a decision or to know how to handle a situation. Frequently, the requests were for other people, that God would meet their specific needs. Sometimes God didn't answer right away. Maybe He wanted to see how committed I was or maybe my timing wasn't His timing, but quite often He answered my specific prayers quickly.

Several years ago, I was in a car accident (yes, it was my fault). I was at a total standstill in the middle of the road when I saw car lights heading toward me. As I heard tires squealing, metal crunching, and glass shattering, I sent up a very short, specific prayer. "Lord, save me!" was the only thing I had time to pray before being hit directly in my car door. Miraculously, neither I nor the other driver was injured. God heard my quick, specific prayer and answered immediately.

Intercessory prayer

Intercessory prayer is the concept of praying for others. Engaging in this type of prayer keeps our prayer life from becoming self-focused. God has given us the responsibility to pray for others (Acts 8:15; Romans 1:10; 2 Corinthians 1:11). We are to pray for our families, friends, leaders, and the lost. Remembering all of these people and their needs seems overwhelming (hence Paul's admonition to pray without ceasing). One way I have found to do this is to offer short prayers for people I come in contact with or those God brings to my mind. We may never see the answers to our prayers for others, but we have confidence that He will answer them.

As we make prayer a part of our lives, we will experience God's presence and power in tangible ways. Bill Hybels, in his book, *Too Busy Not to Pray,* states that if we are willing to invite God into our daily lives through prayer, we will experience His prevailing power in our homes, relationships, schools, and churches. Hybels writes:

> That power may come in the form of wisdom-an idea you desperately need and can't come up with yourself. It may come in the form of courage greater than you could ever muster. It may come in the form of confidence or

perseverance, uncommon staying power, a changed attitude toward a spouse or a child or a parent, changed circumstances, maybe even outright miracles. However it comes, God's prevailing power is released in the lives of people who pray.[4]

Study God's Word

One of my purposes for writing this book was to help people know more about the Bible, but don't look at this book as a replacement for personal Bible reading and study. Through the Bible, we get to know God and His Son more intimately. We learn His character, His will, and His ways. As we read the promises He has made to His people, we learn to live with confidence that He is in control.

Every issue that we face today is either directly or indirectly addressed in the Bible.[5] Just as prayer should be practiced daily, Bible reading and study should also be done consistently. Look for a Bible that is written in contemporary language and start reading. You may want to find a daily or weekly reading plan to follow. Become involved in Bible studies at your church. If you are not able to attend a group study in person, there are many studies now available for purchase or to download as books, workbooks, videos, and podcasts. Look for studies that center on the Bible as the primary source. Learning the Bible is easier now than ever before. There is no excuse for us to remain ignorant of God's truth. Finally, begin memorizing verses that you find especially meaningful. David wrote, *"I have stored up your word in my heart, that I might not sin against you"* (Psalm 119:11 [ESV]).

Fellowship with Other Christians

In a poem by the same name, minister and poet John Dunne (1571-1631) wrote, "No man is an island unto himself." This is especially true for Christians. We are called to live in fellowship with other believers. In Acts 2:42-47, we see the early Christians forming communities, sharing food and possessions with each other. At this time, they were living in fear and uncertainty. They needed the encouragement and protection of being with others who shared their faith. The result was that they not only survived, but they also thrived. We read, *"the Lord added to their number daily those who were being saved"* (vs 47).

We find similar fellowship within the local church. The church is where we grow in knowledge, use the gifts and talents God has given us to serve others, as well as give and receive encouragement. The apostle Paul encouraged the believers at Corinth, saying, *"Now you are the body of Christ, and each one of you is a part of it"* (1 Corinthians 12:27). Also, as we live out our faith in an unbelieving world, it is important that we have others who can encourage us and stand with us in the face of opposition. Ecclesiastes 4:12 reminds us that *"though one may be overpowered, two can defend themselves. A cord of three strands is not quickly broken."* When the world tries to attack our faith, fellow believers are there to stand and fight with us.

The Christian life is exciting, challenging, and at times difficult, but God promises to be with us every step of the way. He tells us, *"I will never leave you or forsake you"* (Joshua 1:5). As we prepare to stand for God, let's grow deep roots so that we may handle every challenge and situation with grace.

Part 3 Chapter 2

STANDING AT HOME - OUR DAILY WITNESS

Dorothy in the *Wizard of Oz* chanted, "There's no place like home." I agree. I love being at home with my family. I enjoy the solitude and peace that my home outside the city provides. Even though I love traveling, I love coming back home even more. For some, though, home is anything but peaceful. Maybe there is chaos in your home from the sheer number of people living there. Maybe you are living with rebellious teens or controlling in-laws. Maybe your relationship with your spouse is less than ideal. Regardless of the tone and temperament of our homes and families, this is where our stand for God begins. It is where we have the unique opportunity to model Christ's love to those we live with every day. The Bible tells us to *"seek to lead a quiet life, to mind your own business, and to work with your own hands...so that you may walk properly in the presence of outsiders and not be dependent on anyone"* (1 Thessalonians 4:11,12 [HCSB]). Matthew 5:16 adds, *"In the same way, let your light shine before others, that they may see your good deeds and glorify your Father in heaven."*

The Bible tells us that Jesus left His home around the age of 30 and spent three years traveling, teaching, and healing. Each time He returned home, He was met by people who would not believe His message. Even His own brothers questioned His claims, but God provided another family for Jesus to be a part of during these trying years. The home of three siblings – Mary, Martha, and Lazarus - became Jesus' "home away from home." There, He found companionship, acceptance, and home-cooked food. He was even called on to settle a dispute between sisters.

Mary and Martha were quite different in their approaches to life. Mary was quiet, reflective, and loved to learn. She would sit and listen to Jesus teach for hours. Martha, on the other hand, was a worker. She was the one making sure the bed was made, dinner ready, and towels set out for Jesus to use. These two sisters demonstrate for us two aspects of witnessing within our homes – attitude and service.

Sharing Jesus Through our Attitudes

Before we dive into our discussion about attitude, let's do a quick check-up. Would people describe you as Scrooge or Santa Claus? When the phone rings, do you expect to hear good news or bad news? Could you be described as a "fountain of joy" or as one of God's "frozen chosen?" And would you say that your attitude draws people to you or does it repel them?

Our attitudes are always on display whether we like it or not. We may be able to fake it for a short time, but eventually our true colors will shine. Jesus' attitude was on display as He interacted with people. He showed patience and a gentle spirit with everyone He met. Even those who didn't accept who He was recognized that He was different. We cannot have these attitudes through our own self-will. When we accept Jesus as our Savior, the Holy Spirit comes to live in our hearts. The Bible tells us that the Holy Spirit is given to instruct, remind, and convict regarding sin (John 16:7-16). He is our comforter and advocate before God. He also brings into our lives characteristics, or attitudes, that allow us to live the way God intends. These "fruits" are given to us when we become Christians. If we rely on God, He will develop these traits. They include love, joy, peace, patience, kindness, goodness, faithfulness, gentleness, and self-control (Galatians 5:22-23). The first three traits – love, joy, and peace – are internal attitudes that provide the foundation for our attitudes toward everything.

Love

Love is the first fruit listed, as it is the foundation for everything else. Jesus commanded His disciples to love, saying, *"By this everyone will know that you are my disciples, if you love one another"* (John 13:35). Paul describes love in 1 Corinthians 13:4-8:

Love is patient, love is kind. It does not envy, it does not boast, it is not proud. It does not dishonor others, it is not self-seeking, it is not easily angered, it keeps no record of wrongs. Love does not delight in evil but rejoices with the truth. It always protects, always trusts, always hopes, always perseveres. Love never fails.

One of the more popular songs of the 1960's told us, *"What the world needs now is love, sweet love. It's the only thing that there's just too little of."*[1] People still need that love today. They need your love and they need Jesus' love. Beth Moore describes the love God wants us to share with others as "audacious," bold and daring. She writes, "The most effective gospel is show and tell. You share Jesus with your heart by the way you love, with your hands by the things you do, and yes, of course, you share Jesus with your mouth. Sooner or later, you won't be able to keep from it. Audacious love unties the shiest tongue."[2]

Joy

Joy can be described as a calmness, contentment, and gladness that goes to the very core and cannot be shaken. At Jesus' birth, the angels proclaimed glad tidings of great joy! This emotion is not to be confused with happiness, because happiness is situational and can change when circumstances change. For example, when everything is going well, I am happy, but when problems arise, happiness turns to unhappiness. Joy is different. It is based on faith and an assurance that God is in control. It is abiding and can withstand the storms of life.

Peace

The third internal attitude given by the Holy Spirit is peace. Peace is a feeling of calmness, freedom from worry, and freedom from strife. Jesus, the Prince of Peace, said, *"Peace I leave with you; my peace I give you. I do not give to you as the world gives. Do not let your hearts be troubled and do not be afraid"* (John 14:27). He provided an illustration of this peace when the disciples' boat was being battered by a storm. He walked on the water out to the disciples while the storm was still raging, and said, *"Take courage, it is I; do not be afraid"* (Matthew 14:27).

We will always have challenges, but we have peace when we acknowledge that nothing can happen to us without God's permission. He has everything under control.

As we live out the internal attitudes of love, joy, and peace, others will see a difference in us. Esther Burroughs describes the witness we share when we live out the internal attitudes of love, joy, and peace in her book, *Splash the Living Water*:

> Mildred McWhorter, a missionary in the inner city of Houston, Texas was saying good-bye to the children for the day. The little boy she was holding in her arms looked up into her eyes, and said: "Miss 'Quater, are you God?"
> She drew back in surprise as she continued to hold him and said, "Oh, no, I'm not God...but God's love lives in my heart."
> "No!" the little guy insisted, "You are God!"
> Taking another deep breath, she said, "Oh, no! I am not God, but His Son, Jesus, lives in my heart."
> As he pointed to her heart, the little boy insisted again, "Oh, no. I can see Him right there."[3]

Sharing Jesus Through our Actions

With the foundational attitudes of love, joy, and peace in place, we move on to those attitudes that affect how we interact with others, namely the outward attitudes of patience, kindness, goodness, and faithfulness. It is through these "fruits" of the Holy Spirit that we become a living model of Christ, demonstrating His love toward others. It is through these attitudes that people are drawn to us and are willing to hear the life-changing message of the gospel.

Patience

One day several years ago, a friend of mine told her four-year-old son that they would be leaving soon to go to McDonald's for lunch. As they walked to the car, a neighbor approached and started a conversation. Ever polite, my friend talked with her for several minutes. Occasionally, her son would tap her on the arm or clear his throat in an effort to remind her of their lunch. Each time, she would calmly say, "Thank you for being patient." Finally, after a lengthy discussion, the neighbor left. As my friend turned to look at her son, he put his hands on his hips and said, "I know, I know, I have been very, very, very patient. What does patient mean anyway?" Patience, or "long-suffering," as some version of the Bible refer to it, is defined as the ability to endure waiting or pain calmly and without complaint.[4] Gary Chapman describes patience as "allowing someone to be imperfect"[5] Developing patience isn't easy. We often get impatient in our quest for patience. Gary Chapman writes that it begins with one choice followed by another until a beautiful habit is formed. He asks, "What would your relationships be like if you…

- Treated everyone, including yourself, as a person in process rather than as a machine that performs?
- Showed in your words and actions that you valued relationships more than time?

- Listened long enough to understand what another person was thinking and feeling?

- Gave up harsh and condemning words and learned to speak softly?

- Focused on finding solutions to problems rather than finding someone to blame?[6]

Jesus modeled patience as He interacted with His disciples. When James and John asked to be given seats beside Jesus in heaven, He calmly explained that it was not up to Him to decide such things. Hearing this request, the other disciples became indignant. Jesus gently reminded them, *"You know that those who are recognized as rulers of the Gentiles lord it over them...but it is not this way among you"* (Mark 10:42-43). In Matthew 26, we read that just hours before His arrest, Jesus went to the Garden of Gethsemane to pray. He asked His three dearest disciples, Peter, James, and John, to go and keep watch with Him. After a period of agonizing prayer, Jesus returned and found the men sleeping. He asked them, *"You could not keep watch with me for one hour?"* This pattern was repeated three times, each time Jesus finding His closest friends asleep. Scripture indicates that Jesus did not grow angry or impatient with them. He simply said, *"Behold, the hour is at hand...let us be going; behold, the one who betrays me is at hand!"* (vs 45-46).

Kindness and goodness

How do we show Christ's love to others? We do it through kindness and goodness. These two characteristics shine like beacons in a dark world of cynicism and self-centeredness. Kindness can stop hatred in its tracks. Chapman defines kindness as "the joy of meeting someone else's needs before your own simply for the sake of the relationship."[7] The apostle Paul writes, *"Therefore, as God's chosen people, holy and dearly loved, clothe yourselves with compassion, kindness, humility, gentleness and patience"* (Colossians 3:12). I love the image of being clothed with kindness, putting it on each morning as I get dressed. An attitude of kindness communicates to others, "You are a person of value."

When was the last time you did something with no thought of getting something in return? Several years ago, the idea of performing "random acts of kindness" became popular. People looked for opportunities to do things for others, simple things like helping carry groceries, opening doors, and paying for someone's cup of coffee. Saying thank you to the mail carrier, giving up a parking spot to a mother with small children, and hugging your spouse when they come in the door are simple, yet profound ways of recognizing others and letting them know they are special.

Faithfulness

One of the most significant truths found in the Bible is that of God's faithfulness. We read in Psalm 100:5, *"For the Lord is good and his love endures forever; his faithfulness continues through all generations."* He is the same today as He was yesterday, and He will be the same every day from here on. We have the absolute assurance that He loves us and will always be there for us. Jesus also exemplified faithfulness to His disciples. Knowing that He would be leaving them soon to return to heaven, He assured them that He would not leave them alone. He would prepare a place for them, saying, *"And if I go and prepare a place for you, I will come back and take you to be with me, that you also may be where I am"* (John 14:3). How can we demonstrate that same faithfulness to our family and friends? In a world that touts "every man for himself," how can we model the loyalty of Christ?

Many years ago, a person would begin a career with one company and stay with them until retirement. In return, the company would demonstrate loyalty to the employee in the form of bonuses, retirement plans, and most importantly, continued employment even in difficult times. Today, people change jobs almost as easily as they change clothes and loyalty in the business world is nearly extinct. When we model the trait of faithfulness, we stand in direct contrast to what society has come to expect. Proverbs 17:17 says *"A friend loves at all times, and a brother is born for a time of adversity."* Look for opportunities to demonstrate faithfulness. In your home, follow through on promises. Be available physically and mentally for your children and spouse. In your community, instead of visiting an elderly neighbor once, plan weekly or monthly visits. Consistently volunteer to serve in places of need. Develop long-term relationships and check in on friends who have moved away. Reconnecting with others speaks volumes about how much you care about them.

Special Attitudes for Difficult Situations

No matter how much love and patience we show to others, there will be times when an extra measure of grace is needed. There are people who, because of past experiences or personal needs, require an especially thoughtful approach. In these instances, the qualities of gentleness and self-control allow us to meet the situation with a Christ-like spirit.

Gentleness

Have you ever spent time with someone who exudes gentleness? Everything they do seems thoughtful and sensitive. They never appear harsh or irritable. They have a calmness that makes people want to be around them. Sometimes their gentleness even attracts non-human creatures. Let me explain. As young children, my two older sons were quite different in their personalities and approaches to life. The younger one was exuberant in everything he did. He was full of life and always on the move. The older one was quieter, approaching life with thoughtfulness and reserve. One afternoon, we visited friends whose cat had recently had kittens. As the boys entered the house, the younger one excitedly began chasing the kittens in an attempt to hold one. As you can imagine, the kittens scurried under the sofa and chairs to avoid being caught. My older son chose to sit down in the middle of the floor. After a few minutes, the kittens came out of hiding and climbed into his lap. They responded to his gentle approach.

The Bible calls us to demonstrate gentleness in our dealings with people. First Peter 3:15-16 tells us, *"Always be prepared to give an answer to everyone who asks you to give the reason for the hope that you have. But do this with gentleness and respect, keeping a clear conscience."* When dealing with an angry person, we are reminded that *"a gentle answer turns away wrath"* (Proverbs 15:1).

Jesus demonstrated a spirit of gentleness with everyone He met. He was tender with children, the weak, and the helpless. He was gentle with a widow whose only son had died. Luke 7:13 says that when Jesus saw her, *"he felt compassion for her, and said to her, 'Do not weep.'"* He then raised her son to life and gave him back to his mother. Jesus was also gentle with the rich young ruler who asked Jesus what he needed to do to inherit eternal life. Scripture says that *"looking at him, Jesus felt a love for him"* (Mark 10:21), knowing that the answer would be difficult for the young man to hear. Jesus also demonstrated gentleness with one particular disciple. Thomas had not been with the other disciples when Jesus appeared to them after his resurrection. When they told him that Jesus was alive, Thomas was not able to accept their testimony. He said to them, *"Unless I see in his hand the imprint of the nails, and put my finger into the place of the nails and put my hand into his side, I will not believe"* (John 20:25). What was Jesus' response? He appeared specifically to Thomas, allowing him to touch His hands and side so that he would believe. May we show that same gentleness with those we meet every day.

Self-control

Okay, I saved the hardest trait for last. For most of us, self-control is difficult. We start the morning with good intentions, but the daily annoyances and temptations wear away our resolve. By lunchtime, we are eating the things we promised to avoid and yelling at the driver in front of us. Why is self-control so important? Because one moment of losing control in front of others can undermine months of godly witness. It is a fact that the world expects Christians to respond differently than the rest of the world. Any time we fall short of that expectation, others don't see our failure. They think that God has failed – that being a Christian doesn't work. I don't know about you, but that thought motivates me to work harder to control my actions.

How can we maintain self-control in difficult situations? It is only possible through the power of the Holy Spirit working in our lives. Remember John 14:27, when Jesus said, *"My peace I give to you?"* He didn't say, "Work really hard to have peace because people need to see your peace." He knew we couldn't do it on our own. In the same way, Jesus says to us, "My self-control I give to you. Let me give you my restraint and resolve as you handle temptation and frustration. Let my peace rule in your heart." Instead of self-control, we are to demonstrate "Holy Spirit-control."

Fruits in Action

Standing for God in our homes and communities requires putting the fruits of the Spirit into action. In Matthew 25, Jesus told the parable of a king who separated the nations into two groups of people. He told the first group he was giving them an inheritance in the kingdom because they had ministered to him when he was hungry, thirsty, without clothes, and in prison. Confused, the people asked when they had done those things. The king replied, *"Truly I say to you, to the extent that you did it to one of these brothers of mine, even the least of them, you did it to me"* (vs 40). We are called to provide these same services for those in our immediate sphere of influence – our family and friends.

As we prepare to minister, we must make sure we are serving with proper motives. Richard Foster, in his book, *Celebration of Disciple,* warns that it is easy to begin serving for wrong motives.[8] He describes the difference between self-righteous service done through human effort and true service with the following comparisons:

Self-righteous Service	True Service
Comes through human effort	Comes through divine urgings
Is impressed with the "big deal"	Does not distinguish small from large service
Requires external rewards	Is contented in hiddenness
Is highly concerned about results	Is free of the need to calculate results
Picks and chooses whom to serve	Is indiscriminate in ministry
Is affected by moods and whims	Ministers simply and faithfully

Jesus told His disciples in Matthew 6:3-4, *"when you give to the needy, do not let your left hand know what your right hand is doing, so that your giving may be in secret. Then your Father, who sees what is done in secret, will reward you."* Hidden service keeps us from doing things for the wrong reasons – for recognition or rewards.

Daily activities done with pure motives demonstrate God's love to others. In our homes, making time to listen to our spouses and children tells them we value their thoughts and ideas. Clean clothes, a hot meal, and warm hugs communicate that they are special and that home is a place of love and safety. In our communities, simple acts such as taking groceries to a sick neighbor, offering to sit with children so parents can have a night out, and mowing a neighbor's lawn when they are out of town show that you notice them and care about them. These small acts done with a servant's heart will act like a stone being thrown into a lake, creating a ripple effect that will produce results that we may never see.

What about you? What small acts of service can you offer to those around you? Do people know you are a Christian by the things you do? Someone said, "If you were on trial for being a Christian, would there be enough evidence to convict you?" I pray that there would be many eyewitnesses who could testify to numerous examples of your faith in action. Richard Foster encourages us to start each day with a prayer, "Lord Jesus, as it would please you, bring me someone today whom I can serve."[9]

STANDING IN PUBLIC- SPEAK TRUTH

"Spread the Good News!" "Let your voice be heard!" "Preach the Gospel!" We as God's people have been admonished to speak out for God, however, most Christians would prefer to live quietly, showing their devotion to the Lord through their lifestyle rather than their words. They don't want to appear pushy or possibly insult someone by talking about God. They don't want to ruffle feathers or cause controversy.

I'm here to tell you that a silent Christian is an ineffective Christian. While Jesus tells us, *"Let your light so shine before men that they may see your good works and praise your Father who is in heaven"* (Matthew 5:16 [GNT]), that is only a start. He personally demonstrated that we must do more. We must speak the truth out loud in the public arena. During His time on earth, Jesus spoke to the sick (Luke 13), the demon-possessed (Mark 5), and sinners (John 8). He spoke to large groups of people (Matthew 5) and taught in the synagogues (Luke 20). He even confronted the religious and political leaders of His day, calling them out for their pride, arrogance, and hypocrisy (Matthew 23). Following Jesus' example, we must actively share God's message in our homes, communities, and nation. We must be diligent to stay informed on topics that affect people's lives. We must be willing to speak up, vote, and become active in effecting change in our land. Let's take a closer look at this call to action.

Be Informed

First, we as Christians must know what is happening in our world at the local, national, and global level. I had a conversation recently with some friends and the subject of Critical Race Theory (CRT) came up. Several people admitted that they had not heard of CRT, even though it has been in the news for months. This is not unusual. I have heard many arguments (also known as excuses) for not being informed. Here are a few: "The news is too depressing," "There's nothing I can do about it," and "Everyone in politics is corrupt." I believe that most Christians don't make an effort to become knowledgeable about current issues because they don't truly appreciate the danger of remaining uninformed.

How can we stand for God when we don't even know what the issues are? I encourage you to make becoming informed a priority by setting aside some time each week to learn more about current topics. This doesn't mean that you know which celebrity won the current reality competition, or which team won the World Series. It does mean staying up to date on matters related to the economy, education, foreign policy, individual freedoms, and natural disasters requiring humanitarian relief and support. To learn about large-scale issues, you may subscribe to a non-partisan national or state newspaper. Trade journals provide up-to-date information on business and industry trends. Also, it is important to stay informed about what is happening in your community. Local newspapers, message boards, city council meetings, and school board meetings are just a few places where you can learn about issues affecting you and your neighbors.

A warning would be appropriate at this point. Not all news is true and not all topics are relevant. Gossip and "social chatter" are not God-honoring sources of information. The Bible advises us that we are to be as shrewd as snakes while being as innocent as doves (Matthew 10:16). Information should be checked for accuracy, not blindly accepted as fact. When possible, get primary source information rather than second-hand reporting. Be aware of bias in reporting that may inadvertently (or purposefully) influence how information is presented. Consult several different types of news media in order to see the different views surrounding an issue. This knowledge will be useful in building common ground with others, making them more receptive to your ideas.

Know the Truth

It is important to know the issues but it is even more important to know what God has to say about those issues. Earlier, we discussed the importance of reading and studying God's Word. We must also pray for His wisdom and discernment as we study. It isn't enough just to know the truth, you must be able to apply the truth to your own life and circumstances. You also must have wisdom and discernment in how you share this knowledge with others. The saying, "People don't care how much you know until they know how much you care," is certainly applicable here. Ask God to help you take what you have learned to effectively speak truth to others.

Speak Truth

I come from a family of educators. My maternal grandfather, while serving as a pastor in a small Baptist church, supported his family by teaching high school math. My mother taught nursing and my father began his career as a physical education teacher. After a few years of teaching, he moved into an administrative position as the principal of a middle school. He loved his work at the school, arriving well ahead of teachers and students and often staying long after everyone else had gone home, but on Friday afternoons during the months of August to May, he would come home from work and transform (in my young mind) into a superhero.

His costume was a black and white striped shirt, with a whistle around his neck. On Friday nights, my dad was a high school football and basketball referee! He loved sports and thoroughly enjoyed interacting with the players and coaches. As a referee, he was not allowed to "choose sides" or cheer for either team. His job was to enforce the rules of the game and make sure that everything went smoothly. At the start of each season, he spent time reviewing the rule book so that he could pass the exam necessary to be able to serve as a referee that season. He had to know the rules. He had to know the truth. The official's rulebook was that source of truth for the sports of football and basketball.

In the same way, we have God's rule book for life – the Bible. As Christians, we must follow and speak God's truth even if it's unpopular in our society.[1] We have a responsibility to share that truth with others so that the game of life can go more smoothly. To carry the sports analogy a little farther, referees can't do their job from the bleachers or the sidelines. They must be on the field or court where the action is. In the same way, we will not be effective when we remain spectators or fans cheering from the stands. We must be willing to enter the "danger zone" and talk about the issues that need to be addressed.[2]

How should we speak the truth in our world? Are there right or wrong ways to go about it? In the beginning, some of you may only feel comfortable sharing what you are learning with family and close friends. Some may feel more comfortable writing a letter to your congressman or local representative. Whatever your comfort zone, I challenge you to do something. When an issue comes up that impacts you or your family, speak up. Talk to those who have influence to make a difference. Write an opinion piece for your local newspaper. Add a post to an online blog. Eventually, you may find yourself speaking at board meetings or advocating on a larger scale.

As we talk or write about issues, we need to remember two things: First, we must remain aware of and sensitive to our audience. As noted earlier, it is important that we know the various (and often conflicting) viewpoints of major issues. Insensitive words or forcing our views on others can lead to resentment and rejection of our ideas. We must speak from a heart of gentleness rather than anger, humility rather than pride, and love rather than hate. First Corinthians 13:1 warns us that if we speak without an attitude of love, we are a *"noisy gong or a clanging cymbal."* We should speak with a tone of gentleness and respect for others (Proverbs 15:1; 1 Peter 3:15).

Second, we must realize that we will face opposition – not only from the general public who most likely are non-Christian, but also from fellow believers. I don't know about you, but I have pretty thin skin. I get my feelings hurt easily and I want people to like me, but I have to realize that when people criticize or reject me, it isn't me they are rejecting. They are rejecting Jesus. I try to remember the words of Paul in Philippians 4:13, *"I can do all things through Christ who strengthens me"* (NKJV). Paul also wrote that even though he was persecuted, he did not grow discouraged or lose heart (2 Corinthians 4:8-9). Even Jesus was not immune from personal attack. On several occasions, the religious leaders tried to trick Him into saying something they could use against Him (see Matthew 12, Mark 2, Luke 20). On at least one occasion, they became so angry with Jesus that they tried to stone Him (see John 8). Eventually, their accusations and lies led to His crucifixion. I hope that we are never called to face that kind of opposition, but I pray that we will maintain a willing heart to endure any trial that comes from standing firmly for God.

Vote

One of the pillars of America's governmental system is the idea that each citizen has a right to participate in deciding who will govern. Voting is a serious responsibility because elected leaders create the laws and policies we all must live by. I have heard some Christians say that they don't vote because they don't think it matters, that one vote won't make a difference. That couldn't be farther from the truth.

On the website TrustworthyWord.com, someone wrote that the Christian's role in government and politics "is not evangelism or discipleship, but it is a loving action to seek the good of your neighbor, the defenseless, and where you live."[3] Scripture tells us, *"Let no one seek his own good, but the good of his neighbor"* (1 Corinthians 10:24[ESV]) and *"Speak up for those who cannot speak for themselves, for the rights of all who are destitute"* (Proverbs 31:8). Rev. Charles Finney wrote to Christians during the 1800's something we all should remember:

> The time has come that Christians must vote for honest men and take consistent ground in politics…Christians have been exceedingly guilty in this matter. But the time has come when they must act differently…God cannot sustain this free and blessed country which we love and pray for unless the Church will take right ground… It seems sometimes as if the foundations of the nation are becoming rotten, and Christians seem to act as if they think God does not see what they do in politics. But I tell you He does see it, and He will bless or curse this nation according to the course [Christians] take [in politics].[4]

In light of the fact that many Christians do not vote in local and national elections, historian and author David Barton responds, "Christians can largely end what has become known as the 'culture war' if only an additional 25 percent would vote, and vote Biblically."[5]

How then shall we vote? Vote according to the principles found throughout the Bible. The overarching themes that we have studied in this book can be applied to nearly every issue we will face in the voting booth. It is especially important to vote according to the Bible when issues such as the protection of human life (Psalm 139; Jeremiah 1:5; Genesis 9:5-7; Leviticus 19:32) and marriage/family values (Genesis 2:20-24; Matthew 19; Romans 1) are on the ballot. In addition to the issues, we must make an effort to learn as much as possible about those running for office. Don't get focused solely on "party politics." Instead, look deeper than a candidate's party affiliation. What does he believe about key issues? How has she voted in the past? There are many websites available for people to see the voting record of elected officials. Most people running for office will also have a website that highlights their background and stance on pertinent issues. Finally, we need to encourage others to vote. Share with them the facts about the issues and candidates so that they can vote wisely. We may even offer to help them become registered voters.

In recent years, we have seen an increase in mail-in ballots and ballot-harvesting concerns. Some groups have misused these strategies to get more votes for their candidates. Christian organizations may also employ honest and lawful campaigns to "get out the vote." Let's not let our election process be undermined because we weren't willing to reach out to others.

Get Involved

I am going to end this chapter with two additional challenges: First, I urge you to consider running for office. Why is this important? One of the most frequently quoted verses by our nation's founders is, *"When the righteous are in authority, the people rejoice; but when the wicked rule, the people groan"* (Proverbs 29:2[RSV]). But the righteous can't rule unless there are qualified believers who are willing to run for office, and unless the rest of us are willing to elect them when they do run.[6] Christian author Tim LaHaye also encourages Christians to seek office. He writes:

> Pray that an army of God-fearing men and women will be inspired to run for the almost one hundred thousand elective offices of this land on the local, state-wide, and national levels. From school board to city council to state legislature to congress, we need elected officials who realize they are responsible to God for the way they rule their city or this country.[7]

Local elections do not require large amounts of money or time, but the effects are significant. Many of you have expertise in the areas of education, business, finance, and law that are directly related to key issues. Would you consider accepting the challenge of running for office?

The second challenge I issue to everyone is to support those running for office. A few months before the 2020 national elections, Franklin Graham wrote:

> It is our civic responsibility as Christians, and we must do all we can to support candidates on the federal, state and local level who most strongly support Biblical principles.... I hope Christians across the nation realize the grave dangers that are poised to strike at the heart of the religious liberties we have fought so hard to protect.[8]

I encourage you to find ways to support Godly candidates. Donate to their campaigns, volunteer to hand out materials or make phone calls, and share what you know about the candidate with friends and co-workers. Pray for the candidates, asking God to protect and guide them throughout the election process. Pray that He would give them wisdom and discernment as they campaign and serve. Again, it doesn't take a lot of time or money to do these things. What great things can be accomplished if everyone would do just a little.

Christian radio host Bill Arnold offers a note of encouragement for us as we begin to stretch our faith and step out of our comfort zones. He was addressing pastors but his message is appropriate for all Christians. "If we as pastors and Christian leaders would preach, teach, live, exhort the Word of God - bathe it in prayer, but give God's take on all these issues - it would change the world."[9]

And I offer my hearty, "Amen!"

Part 3 Chapter 4

STANDING THROUGH SERVICE

We previously looked at how we can share God's love with our family, friends, and neighbors. This serves as our starting point in standing for God, but I believe we are called to do more, to go beyond our small circle of influence to meet the needs of people across our nation and beyond. God wants to use us to impact others on a larger scale. He calls us to make a difference in the lives of people by uniting with other believers to effect change far beyond our individual abilities. Let's see how.

Christians as "Change Agents"

Earlier, we learned that Christians are a chosen people and a holy nation. As such, God does not intend for us to operate as lone rangers. He calls us to join with others in order to have a bigger impact for Him. The passage goes on to say that we have been called out of darkness into His light but we weren't called into His light only for ourselves. Jonathan Parnell describes our purpose, saying, "God's aim in calling us out of darkness is to send us back to (but not into) that darkness to 'proclaim his excellencies.'"[1]

Our job is to be in the world, but not of the world for the purpose of winning others to Christ. Sounds tricky, doesn't it? Kind of like a recovering alcoholic working in a bar. That's precisely why God urges us to work with other Christians, so that we may be strong in the face of worldly temptations while living as shining examples of Jesus' love. The apostle Peter put it this way, *"Dear friends, I urge you, as foreigners and exiles, to abstain from sinful desires, which wage war against your soul. Live such good lives among the pagans that, though they accuse you of doing wrong, they may see your good deeds and glorify God on the day he visits us"* (1 Peter 2:10-12).

Science is not one of my areas of expertise. In fact, I remember very little of what I learned in school. I do remember studying about catalysts in chemistry. Catalysts, when introduced to other substances, speed up the rate of a reaction without being consumed. They serve as "change agents," stimulating a desired reaction. In the same way, we are called to be change agents for God. As we interact with others, our actions start a process within them that can either draw them towards the gospel or repel them away from anything related to God. The influencing factor is not them, it is us. Os Hillman writes, "the Christian message today has been shut out because of the way we deliver it, not because the message is wrong. We are more known by what we don't like than what we believe. Few people are attracted to Christ through a boycott."[2]

If this is true, how can we best draw people to Christ? First, we attract people by living a positive Christian lifestyle, demonstrating respect for everyone, regardless of the choices they make. We also seek to benefit society by being problem solvers. Jesus modeled this by solving problems everywhere He went, which resulted in His having a greater influence in people's lives. Other change agents in the Bible include Moses, Daniel, and Esther. Each of these people became aware of a problem and was willing to get involved in the situation to effect change.

More contemporary examples of people having a wide influence on society include William Wilberforce, Nelson Mandela, and Martin Luther King, Jr. Each of these men recognized the effects of sin and injustice in the world and determined to make a difference. They were willing to leave their comfort zones to speak and act as lights in the darkness. Their actions led to changes in society, bringing justice and freedom to millions of people.

We are called to do the same, to step out of our comfort zones to make a difference on a large scale. For the remainder of this chapter, I want to highlight several organizations and individuals who are expanding their spheres of influence to reach people outside of their local area. In some cases, many groups join together to effect change on a global level. Others, after identifying a need, started small. Their personal efforts were multiplied as others joined their mission. My purpose in sharing these particular stories is not to suggest that you become part of any specific endeavor, but that you may be inspired to find your own purpose, your own unique mission for sharing God with the world.

Organizations Serving the World

Baptist World Alliance

The Baptist World Alliance (BWA), founded in 1905, is a fellowship of nearly 250 conventions and unions in 128 countries and territories. Their vision is to "empower people of faith to collaboratively support persecuted communities of all faiths, challenge religious repression, and globally expand freedom of religion, belief, and conscience."[3] To that end, they work to impact the world for Christ through worship, fellowship, missions, and evangelism. They respond to the needs of people by providing aid and relief to those in need. They also seek to defend religious freedom and human rights.

One specific ministry of the BWA is 21 Wilberforce, which draws its inspiration from the British parliamentarian William Wilberforce (1759-1833), who led a movement against the slave trade in England. In addition to defending persecuted churches in China, they also provide support and advocacy for women's religious freedom in Africa. Recently, they have worked with people in Afghanistan to evacuate Christians from the country following the takeover by the Taliban. This alliance is truly meeting the needs of Christians in all parts of the world.

Compassion International

Compassion International (CI) is another organization dedicated to the needs of people on a global scale.[4] This church-driven organization focuses specifically on meeting the needs of children, such as food, clothing, medical care, and education. They provide tools for local churches to work with the children in their communities. Through their primary model of sponsorship, Christians are invited to "sponsor" a needy child by providing monthly donations. These funds are then given to the local church in that area to provide children with food, hygiene items, medical care, and opportunities to learn life skills. Members of the churches share the gospel of Jesus with these children while looking out for their safety and personal development. Compassion International currently has over 2.2 million sponsored infants and children in more than 27 countries worldwide.

Navigators

Another organization committed to sharing the gospel is the Navigators.[5] This ministry began in the 1930s, when Dawson Trotman (1906-1956), a young California lumberyard worker, realized how the principles of discipleship had positively impacted his life. He embarked on a mission to teach these same principles to others, eventually forming the Navigators ministry. Their motto, "To know Christ, make Him known, and help others do the same," forms the foundation for sharing the gospel and discipling new believers. The Navigators provide discipleship and support through ministries on college campuses and military bases, as well as with first responders. They also offer Bible studies, personal teaching, and mentoring to people where they live – in inner cities, workplaces, and local communities.

Samaritan's Purse

One additional organization making a difference in the lives of people across the globe is Samaritan's Purse. This nondenominational evangelical Christian organization seeks to "provide spiritual and physical aid to hurting people around the world."[6] Founded in 1970, Samaritan's Purse has helped meet needs of people affected by war, poverty, natural disasters, disease, and famine with the purpose of sharing the gospel. They provide food, medicine, and other assistance to those in need.

One particular activity sponsored by Samaritan's Purse is Operation Christmas Child. Starting in 1993 as a ministry to children in the Balkans, these volunteers fill shoeboxes with toys, personal care items, and clothing and send them to children in other countries, along with literature in their native language introducing them to Jesus. To date, more than 198 million children in more than 170 countries and territories have received an Operation Christmas Child shoebox. According to the Samaritan's Purse website, this project "delivers not only the joy of what, for many kids, is their first gift ever, but also gives them a tangible expression of God's love."

The Local Church in Action

The local church is God's agent for change. One writer noted, "It is not enough for the church to be engaged with the state in healing social ills, though this is important at times. But when the world can turn around and see a group of God's people exhibiting substantial healing in the area of human relationships in their present life, then the world will take notice."[7]

There are many vibrant churches across America who are making an impact for Christ. One such church is Community Christian Church in Chicago, Illinois. This church seeks to meet the needs of members through worship and discipleship.[8] They go beyond the doors of their church, carrying God's love into their community. Their outreach ministry, entitled, Community Cares, seeks to provide relief by meeting the immediate needs of people in their community, to develop people through nurturing relationships, and to provide holistic transformation in the areas of education, race, poverty, and incarceration. They offer after-school programs for children and provide food and support for homeless shelters. They have recently started providing small group studies and weekly services for those in prison, as well as re-entry support and mentoring for families during their transition back home.

Individuals Making a Difference

Sometimes God calls individuals to step out and do something above and beyond daily activities. Each of the following people saw a need and responded as Isaiah did, with *"Here am I, send me"* (Isaiah 6:8). You may have heard of a few of these people, but you will love getting to know more about others.

Jena Lee Nardella and Blood:Water

When Jena Lee Nardella was a student at Whitworth University, she became concerned about the lack of clean water and the prevalence of HIV/AIDS in Africa. She drafted the plans that would ultimately become Blood:Water, the clean-water initiative that she founded in 2004 with the Christian band Jars of Clay. Since that time, her organization has raised over $40 million and worked alongside more than 33 African-led organizations to bring clean water and HIV/AIDS support to communities in more than twelve countries.[9] With the support of Blood:Water, nearly 1 million people have access to safe water, more than 1.1 million people have been trained in proper sanitation and hygiene practices, nearly 700,000 people have been provided HIV prevention service, and nearly 250,000 people have been provided HIV testing and counseling services. Jena has written about her experiences in the book, *One Thousand Wells: How an Audacious Goal Taught Me to Love the World Instead of Save It.*[10] She is currently working to support other social entrepreneurs through the nonprofit organization, *Praxis.*

Kirk Cameron

Kirk Cameron is known by millions as "Mike Seaver" from the 1980's hit sit-com, *Growing Pains*. Since then, he has invested his time and energy into faith and family-focused films, television shows, and live events.[11] He starred in the movie *Fireproof*, a film about the power of faith to save a marriage. Cameron has used his public popularity to produce documentaries and live events focused on marriage, family, and parenting. His newest films focus on the topics of adoption and homeschooling.

Recently, Cameron has been featured in the national media for his American Campfire Revival: 100 Day campaign. This program urges believers and the church to return to the principles that will bring blessing and protection to America. Cameron writes on his website, "My prayer is that the American Campfire Revival will bring new life, courage and strength to the family of faith. Together, we will light fires of revival within the hearts of our families, friends, neighbors, and churches, and as the eyes of the whole world are upon us, they will say, 'May God do for us in our nation as He has done again in America.'"[11]

Thomas Lake

Thomas Lake was raised in a Christian home, the third of six children. His mother homeschooled the children and his father pastored a small charismatic church. Thomas loved to read, favoring history, sports, and the encyclopedia. After college, he began a career as a writer, eventually becoming one of the youngest senior writers at *Sports Illustrated*. Not shy about his Christian faith, his writing seeks to bring human experiences to life. His first magazine story, "2 on 5," won the Henry Luce Award for most outstanding story of 2008 across all Time Inc. publications. His story "The Boy They Couldn't Kill" was named one of the 60 best features in the history of *Sports Illustrated*.[12]

Lake is currently a senior writer for CNN Digital and the author of "Unprecedented: The Election That Changed Everything."[13] When asked about his career, he replied, "I couldn't have predicted that I would wind up in a job that puts me in the mainstream this way. It's been a gradual process, one small step by small step. It's really such an exciting chance that I have to tell these stories that inspire and get the chance for so many people to read them."

Lila Rose

At the age of 15, Lila Rose started Live Action, an organization which encourages young people to join the pro-life movement.[14] Since then, she has become a writer, speaker, and activist. She is responsible for a number of undercover videos that have exposed certain Planned Parenthood practices. Her investigations into the abortion industry have been featured in news publications such as the *Los Angeles Times* and the *Washington Post*, as well as on most major news stations.

Lila speaks internationally on family and cultural issues and has addressed members of the European Parliament and spoken at the United Nations' Commission on the Status of Women. She has been named among *National Journal's* "25 Most Influential Washington Women Under 35," and *Christianity Today's* "33 under Thirty-Three."

Katie Stagliano and Katie's Krops

My final individual to highlight is especially dear to me. In the same town where we raised our children, a nine- year-old girl was given a tiny cabbage seedling as part of her school's Bonnie Plants Third Grade Cabbage Program. Katie Stagliano tended that little seedling until it grew to a 40 pound head of cabbage. She then donated the cabbage to a soup kitchen where it helped to feed over 275 people. That led Katie to start vegetable gardens for the purpose of donating the harvest to help feed people in need.[15]

Katie's Krops now has 100 gardens growing across the country and has donated thousands of pounds of fresh produce to families, hunger-relief programs, and cancer centers. They also provide free meals to people in need. According to their website, the mission of Katie's Krops is to empower youth to start and maintain vegetable gardens of all sizes and donate the harvest to help feed people in need, as well as to assist and inspire others to do the same. They write, "The problem of hunger is real, Katie's Krops mission is simple, we all can help because...It only takes a seedling!"

As we conclude our time together, I encourage you to ask God to reveal His plans for you. I know He has specific things that only you can do to minister His grace to others. He may reveal His plan through new ideas that come to your mind, desires that unfold in your heart, and doors of opportunity that miraculously open. Regardless of what you are called to do, always be mindful that God is in control. He doesn't need you or me to accomplish His purpose. Rather, He calls us to be participants with Him, allowing us the privilege of serving Him by serving others. Our responsibility is to be faithful to the call. He will bring the harvest. Let us remember that the weight of the future is not on our shoulders. Christ is still Lord, and He is still on the throne.

We began our study with the verse, *"Blessed is the nation whose God is the Lord"* (Psalm 33:12). I would like to close with the remaining verses from this psalm. To God be the glory!

Behold, the eye of the Lord is on those who fear him,
  on those who hope in his steadfast love,
that he may deliver their soul from death
  and keep them alive in famine.
Our soul waits for the Lord;
  he is our help and our shield.
For our heart is glad in him,
  because we trust in his holy name.
Let your steadfast love, O Lord, be upon us,
  even as we hope in you. (vs 18-22, [ESV])

Reference

Introduction Part 1

1. Brian Duignan, "Basic Tenets of Critical Race Theory," *Encyclopedia Britannica,* (accessed March 20, 2023), https://www.britannica.com/topic/critical-race-theory/Basic-tenets-of-critical-race-theory

2. Stephen Sawchuk, "What is Critical Race Theory and Why is It Under Attack?," *Education Week,* May 18, 2021, https://www.edweek.org/leadership/what-is-critical-race-theory-and-why-is-it-under-attack/2021/05.

3. "Climate," *CNN* online, accessed June 15, 2022, https://www.cnn.com/specials/world/cnn-climate.

4. "Fentanyl." *Centers for Disease Control and Prevention* online, June 1, 2022,https://www.cdc.gov/opioids/basics/fentanyl.html.

5. "Human Trafficking: Key Statistics and Resources," *Deliverfund* online, (accessed January 3, 2023), https://deliverfund.org/the-human-trafficking-problem-in-america/human-trafficking-statistics-and-resources/?gclid=Cj0KCQiAtvSdBhD0ARIsAPf8oNlFnR6LHOFSb78avYY AHO89g_jVk2XScgVTEA07lSOn2Biz6oW3jcYaAm-gEALw_wcB.

6. Nick Timiraos, "Fed Raises Rates by 0.75 Percentage Point, Largest Increase Since 1994," *Wall Street Journal,* June 15, 2022, https://www.wsj.com/articles/fed-raises-rates-by-0-75-percentage-point-largest-increase-since-1994-11655316170.

7. "Divorce Rate by State," *World Population Review* online,(accessed May 13, 2022),https://worldpopulationreview.com/state-ranking/divorce-rate-by-state.

8. Benjamin Gurrentz and Tayelor Valerio, "More than 190,000 Children Living With Two Same-Sex Parents in 2019," *Census.gov* online, Nov 19, 2019, https://www.census.gov/library/stories/2019/11/first-time-same-sex-couples-in-current-population-survey-tables.html.

9. "Read the Supreme Court's Full Opinion Overturning Roe v Wade," *PBS* online, June 24, 2022, https://www.pbs.org/newshour/politics/read-the-supreme-courts-full-opinion-overturning-roe-v-wade.

10. "Cancel Culture," *Merriam-Webster*.com (accessed June 25, 2022), https://www.merriam-webster.com/dictionary/ cancel%20culture.

11. "Current Threats to Religious Liberties," *United States Conference of Catholic Bishops* website, (accessed May 15, 2022), https://www.usccb.org/committees/religious-liberty/current-threats-religious -liberty.

Chapter 1 Part 1

1. David Jaffee, "Religion and Culture in North America, 1600–1700." In *Heilbrunn Timeline of Art History*. New York: The Metropolitan Museum of Art, 2000–, October 2002, http://www.metmuseum.org/toah/hd/recu/hd_recu.htm.

2. Patrick J. Kiger. "7 Events That Enraged Colonists and Led to the American Revolution," *History.com*, updated September 22, 2022, https://www.history.com/news/american-revolution-causes.

3. David Barton (a), *America's Godly Heritage,* (Aledo, TX: Wallbuilders Press, 2016), 8-9.

4 Tim LaHaye, *Faith of Our Founding Fathers*, (Green Forest, AZ: Master Books, Inc., 2000), 111.

5. David Barton (b), *The Role of Pastors and Christians in Civil Government* (Aledo, TX: Wallbuilders Press, 2016), p. 30.

6. David Barton (a), *ibid.,* 20.

7. David Barton (b), *ibid.,* 23.

8. "Quotations on the Jefferson Memorial," *Thomas Jefferson Monticello* online, (accessed January 13, 2023), https://www.monticello.org/research-education/thomas-jefferson-encyclopedia/quotations-jefferson-memorial/.

9. David Barton (b), *ibid.,* 29.

10. David Barton (b), *ibid.,* 28.

11. Tim LaHaye, *ibid.,* 137.

12. U.S. Constitution, preamble.

13. David Barton (b), *ibid.,* 22.

14. Tim LaHaye, *ibid.,* 71-72.

15. David Barton (a), *ibid.,* 30.

16. David Barton (b), *ibid.,* 11.

17. Mary Wisniewski, "Religion and Controversy, Always Part of U.S. Education," *U.S. News* online, June 9, 2011, https://www.reuters.com/article/us-usa-

religion-schools/religion-and-controversy-always-part-of-u-s-education-idUSTRE75829R20110609.

18. "The Star-Spangled Banner," StarSpangledMusic.com, (accessed June 11, 2022), https://starspangledmusic.org/the-star-spangled-banner-correct.

19. "My Country, "Tis of Thee," *Gilder Lehrman Institute of American History* online, (accessed November 24, 2022), https://www.gilderlehrman.org/history-resources/spotlight-primary-source/my-country-tis-hee?gclid=CjwKCAiAyfybBhBKEiwAgtB7fsiaUT_XJ81LcMWGlYO3edTah9 7d8BtGpz9lVu1yM6d3ROX3GfMbTBoCF1UQAvD_BwE.

20. Kerby Anderson, "God in Our Nation's Capital," *Probe* online, January 29, 2007, https://probe.org/god-in-our-nations-capital.

Chapter 3 Part 1

1. "Who is the Blessed Nation of Psalm 33:12?" *Teaching the Word Ministries* online, (accessed May 15, 2022), http://www.teachingtheword.org/apps/articles/?blogid=5449&articleid=8580 2.

2. David Palmer, "Blessed Is the Nation Whose God is the Lord," *Kent Methodist* online, July 5 2016, https://www.kentmethodist.org/blessed-nation-whose-god-lord/.

3. Benjamin Franklin, *Constitutional Convention Address on Prayer* (speech, June 28, 1787, Philadelphia, PA), *American Rhetoric* online, (accessed November 12, 2022), https://www.americanrhetoric.com/speeches/benfranklin.htm.

4. Samuel Adams, "Proclamation For a Day of Public Fasting, Humiliation and Prayer," (speech, February 28, 1795), *Revolutionary War and Beyond* online, (accessed May 14, 2022), https://www.revolutionary-war-and-beyond.com/Samuel-adams-proclamation-february-28-1795.html.

5. Franklin Graham, "Last Call for America?" *DecisionMagazine* online, November 1, 2020, https://decisionmagazine.com/franklin-graham-last-call-for-americ

Chapter 1 Part 2

1. Martin G. Collins, "What the Bible Says About God's Standard of Morality," *Forerunner Commentary* [posted on BibleTools.org],(accessed April 23, 2022), https://www.bibletools.org/index.cfm/fuseaction/topical.show/RTD/cgg/I D/13631/Gods-Standard-Morality.htm.

2. Lance Ponder, "Creative Science: Morality," *Bible.org*, (accessed May 15, 2022), https://bible.org/seriespage/35-morality.

3. Lance Ponder, *ibid.*

4. David Kinnaman and Gabe Lyons, "Six Principles of a Jesus-Centered Moral Order," *The Laymen* online, March 9, 2016, https://layman.org/six-principles-of-a-jesus-centered -moral-order/.

5. Billy Graham, "Answers: 'Why Can't People Live Life the Way They Want?'" *Billy Graham Evangelistic Association* online, June 22, 2019, https://billygraham.org/answer/Why-cant-people-live-life-the-way-they-want-to-when-it-comes-to-their-own-personal-morality/.

6. Billy Graham. *ibid.*

Chapter 2 Part 2

1.Tony Robbins, "What is Leadership?" *TonyRobbins.com*, (accessed August 20, 2022), https://www.tonyrobbins.com/what-is-leadership/.

2.Rick Warren, "The Leadership America Needs," *Christian Post Report* online, November 4, 2008 https://www.christianpost.com/news/the-leadership-america-needs.html.

3.Rick Warren, *ibid.*

Chapter 3 Part 2

1. Margaret Thatcher, 'Quotes," *GoodReads.com*, (accessed November 14, 2022), https://www.goodreads.com/quotes/2914-no-one-would-remember-the-good-samaritan-if-he-d-only-had.

2. Charles Swindoll, *Active Spirituality*, (Dallas, TX: Word Publishing, 1994), 73.

3. "Greed," *Merriam-Webster Dictionary* online, (accessed June 6, 2022) https://www.merriam-webster.com/dictionary/greed.

4. "What Does the Bible Say About Christian Values and Christian Life?" *Christian Bible Reference* online, (accessed April 14, 2022). https://www.christianbiblereference.org/faq_ChristianValues.htm.

5. "Charity," *Merriam-Webster Dictionary* online, (accessed June 6, 2022),https://www.merriam-webster.com/dictionary/charity.

6. "How Welfare Began in the United States," *Constitutional Rights Foundation* online, (accessed July 7, 2022), https://www.crf-usa.org/bill-of-rights-in-action/bria-14-3-a-how-welfare-began-in-the-united-states.html.

7. John Hagee, "Power to Transform Society," *The Life Plan Study Bible,* (Nashville, TN, Thomas Nelson, Inc., 2004), 1182.

8. Avery Foley, "Top Four Biblical Reasons Not to Panic about Climate Change," *Answers in Genesis* online, February 20, 2020, https://answersingenesis.org/environmental-science/climate-change/climate-change-and-the-bible/.

Chapter 4 Part 2

1. Ronald Reagan, "Inaugural Address," (speech, Sacramento, CA, January 5,1967), *Reagan Library* online, https://www.reaganlibrary.gov/archives/speech/january-5-1967-inaugural-address-public-ceremony.

2. Billy Graham, "5 Pieces of Marriage Advice From Billy and Ruth Graham," *Billy Graham Evangelistic Association* online, February 4, 2022, https://billygraham.org/story/5-pieces-of-marriage-advice-from-billy-and-ruth-graham/.

3. A. H. Maslow, "A Theory of Human Motivation," *Psychological Review,* 50,4, (accessed August 18, 2022), https://doi.org/10.1037/h0054346.

4. John W. Ritenbaugh, "Leadership and Covenants, Part 6," (sermon, The Church of the Great God, Fort Mill, SC , January 23, 2016), https://www.cgg.org/index.cfm/library/sermon/id/3805/leadership-and-covenants-part-six.htm.

5. Lance Ponder, "Creative Science: Morality," *Bible.org*, (accessed May 15, 2022), https://bible.org/seriespage/35-morality.

6. Joshua Harris, *I Kissed Dating Goodbye,* (Sisters, OR: Multnomah Books,1997), 93.

7. "Discipline," *Merriam-Webster Dictionary* online, (accessed May 25, 2022), https://www.merriam-webster.com/dictionary/discipline.

8. Lance Ponder, *ibid.*

9 Pope John Paul II, "Homily of John Paul II," (homily, Perth, Australia, November 30, 1986, https://www.vatican.va/content/john-paul-ii/en/homilies/1986/documents/hf_jp-ii_hom_19861130_perth-australia.html.

Chapter 5 Part 2

1. "Great Wall of China," *Encyclopedia Britannica* online, (accessed September 2, 2022), https://www.britannica.com/topic/Great-Wall-of-China.

2. "Walls of Babylon," *Global Security* online, (accessed September 2, 2022), https://www.globalsecurity.org/military/world/168ut168/168ut168lon-walls.htm,).

3. "What does the Bible teach about serving your country?" *Word at Work* online, (accessed September 3, 2022), https://www.wordatwork.org.uk/answers/what-does-bible-teach-about-serving-your-country.

4. Jack Wellman, "Top 7 Bible Verses about the Military," *Patheos* online, March 17, 2016, https://www.patheos.com/blogs/christiancrier/2016/03/17/top-7-bible-verses-about-military/.

5. George W Bush, "President Delivers State of the Union Address." *Whitehouse Archives* online, January 29, 2002, https://georgewbush-whitehouse.archives.gov/news/releases/2002/01/20020129-11.html.

6. "Evangelical Leaders Say the Bible Influences Their Views on Foreign Policy," *National Association of Evangelicals* online, January 28, 2021, https://www.nae.org/bible-influences-foreign-policy/.

Chapter 6 Part 2

1. Caleb Mathis, "What Does the Bible Say about Race?" *Crossroads Church.net*, (accessed September 3, 2022), https://www.crossroads.net/media/articles/race-through-the-bible-part-1-the-old-testament.

2. Caleb Mathis, *ibid.*

3. Timothy Keller, "The Bible and Race," *Gospel in Life* online, Spring 2020, https://quarterly.gospelinlife.com/the-bible-and-race.

4. Todd Wilson, "More than Imago Dei," *Pastor Theologians* online, (accessed September 10, 2022), https://www.pastortheologians.com/articles/2020/9/1/more-than-imago-dei.

5. Caleb Mathis, *ibid.*

6. Matthew Soerens, "What Does the Bible Say About Refugees?" *Lifeway Research* online, May 20, 2022, https://research.lifeway.com/2022/05/20/what-does-the-bible-say-about-refugees/.

7. Aaron Earls, "10 Countries With the Largest Christian Populations," *Lifeway Research* online, May 2, 2019, https://research.lifeway.com/2019/04/02/10-countries-with-the-largest-christian-populations/.

8. "Countries Where Christianity Is Illegal 2023," *World Population Review* online, (accessed January 15, 2023), https://worldpopulationreview.com/country-rankings/countries-where-christianity-is-illegal.

9. Matthew Soerens, *ibid.*

10. Mark Coppenger, "The Bible and Health Care," *BibleMesh* online, November 13, 2013, *https://biblemesh.com/blog/the-bible-and-health-care/*.

11. Neil Mammen, *40 Days Towards a More Godly Nation,* (San Jose, CA: Rational Free Press-American Family Association, 2014), 289.

12. Ashley Evans, "Bible Verses About Education," *BibleReasons.com*, December 20, 2022 https://biblereasons.com/education/.

Chapter 1 Part 3

1. Rick Warren, *The Purpose-Driven Life,* (Grand Rapids, MI: Zondervan, 2002), 17.

2. "Ambassador," *Merriam-Webster Dictionary* online, (accessed July 8, 2022), https://www.merriam-webster.com/dictionary/ambassador.

3. Greg Laurie, *Tell Someone: You Can Share the Good News,* (Nashville, TN: B & H Publishing, 2016), 10

4. Bill Hybels, *Too Busy Not to Pray: Slowing Down to Be with God,* (Downers Grove, IL, InterVarsity Press, 1998), 15.

5. Bill Arnold, "Scripture: The Ultimate Change Agent," *Early Morning Late Show* (podcast), July 26, 2017, https://myfaithradio.com/2017/scripture-ultimate-change-agent/.

Chapter 2 Part 3

1. "What the World Needs Now is Love," *Lyrics.com*, STANDS4 LLC, 2023, (accessed January 4, 2023), https://www.lyrics.com/lyric/15554939/Burt+Bacharach/What+the+World+Needs+Now+Is+Love.

2. Beth Moore, *Audacious,* (Nashville, TN: B&H Publishing Group, 2015), 144.

3. Esther Burroughs, *Splash the Living Water,* (Nashville, TN: Thomas Nelson Publishers, 1999), 61.

4. "Patience," *Merriam-Webster Dictionary* online, (accessed June 6, 2022), https://www.merriam-webster.com/dictionary/patience.

5. Gary Chapman, *Love as a Way of Life: Seven Keys to Transforming Every Area of Your Life,* (Colorado Springs, CO: Waterbrook Press, 2008), 43.

6. Gary Chapman, *ibid.,* 63.

7. Gary Chapman, *ibid,* 18.

8. Richard J. Foster, *Celebration of Discipline: The Path to Spiritual Growth,* (San Francisco, CA: Harper & Row Publishers, 1988), 128-129.

9. Richard J. Foster, *ibid,* 140.

Chapter 3 Part 3

1. "Does the Bible Say Anything About Our Vote?" *Baptist 21.com* (blog), November 1, 2012, https://baptist21.com/blog-posts/2012/does-the-bible-say-anything-about-our-vote-2/.

2. Bill Arnold, "Scripture: The Ultimate Change Agent," *Early Morning Late Show* (podcast, July 26, 2017), https://myfaithradio.com/2017/scripture-ultimate-change-agent/.

3. "What does the Bible Say about Voting and Politics?" *TrustworthyWord.com,* (accessed May 15, 2022), https://www.trustworthyword.com/what-does-the-bible-say-about-

voting-and-politics.

4. David Barton, *The Role of Pastors and Christians in Civil Government,* (Aledo, TX: Wallbuilders Press, 2016), 36.

5. David Barton, *ibid.,* 34.

6. David Barton, *ibid.,* 37.

7. Tim LaHaye, *Faith of Our Founding Fathers,* (Green Forest, AZ: Master Books, Inc., 2000), 200.

8. Franklin Graham, "Blessed is the Nation Whose God is the Lord,"

DecisionMagazine.com; September 21, 2020, https://decisionmagazine.com/franklin-graham-blessed-is-the-nation-whose-god-is-the-lord/.

9. Bill Arnold, *ibid.*

Chapter 4 Part 3

1. Jonathan Parnell, "Six Truths on Christian Involvement in Society," *Cities Church* online, (sermon, Cities Church, June 19, 2011), https://www.citieschurch.com/sermons.

2. "Be Agents of Change," *The Just Life* online, September 14, 2010, https://thejustlife.org/3-be-agents-of-change-59b46667af53.

3. "Baptist World Alliance," *Baptist World* online, (accessed September 14, 2022), https://baptistworld.org/mission-vision/.

4. "Compassion International," *Compassion International* online, (accessed September 14, 2022), https://www.compassion.com/about/about-us.htm.

5. "Navigators," *Navigators* online, (accessed September 15, 2022), https://www.navigators.org/about/.

6. "Samaritan's Purse," *Samaritan's Purse* online, (accessed September 15, 2022), *https://www.samaritanspurse.org/our-ministry/about-us/*.

7. "Be Agents of Change," *ibid.*

8. Community Christian Church, *Community Christian* online, https://communitychristian.org/cares/, (accessed September 20, 2022).

9. "Blood:Water," *Blood:Water* online, (accessed September 20, 2022), https://bloodwater.org/.

10. "Jena Lee Nardella," *Jena Lee Nardella* online, (accessed September 12, 2022), http://www.jenaleenardella.com/.

11. "Kirk Cameron," *Kirk Cameron* online, (accessed December 13, 2022), https://www.kirkcameron.com/.

12. "Thomas Lake," *CNN* online, (accessed October 7, 2022), https://www.cnn.com/profiles/thomas-lake-profile.

13. Owen Strachan, "The Finest Young Sportswriter in America," *The Gospel Coalition* online, October 6, 2014, https://www.thegospelcoalition.org/article/the-finest-young-sportswriter-in-america/.

14 "Meet Lila Rose," *Live Action* online, (accessed January 2, 2023), https://www.liveaction.org/media/meet-lila-rose/.

15. "Katie's Krops," *Katie's Krops* online, (accessed December 20, 2022), https://katieskrops.com/.

Other Books by the Author:

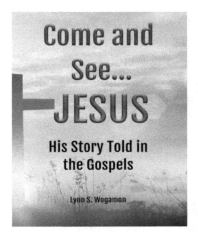

Come and See…Jesus

ISBN: 9781663591975

Come and see! The very words spark curiosity and excitement. When we receive this invitation, we immediately expect to find something wonderful. And when we ourselves have experienced something exciting, we eagerly share it with others.

Jesus spoke the words "come and see…" to people he met as he journeyed during his time on earth. He invited them to see him and his truth as God's Son. Others, after having seen Jesus for themselves, called to friends and family to "come and see". And all who saw Jesus were changed forever.

Come and See…Jesus tells the story of Jesus from his birth through his ascension as presented in the gospels of Matthew, Mark, Luke, and John. This paraphrase of the gospels allows readers to walk with Jesus during his time on earth, learning who he is and why he came to earth in human form.

Words for a Young Heart
ISBN: 9781666221039

The Bible tells children about God and His love for them. Words for a Young Heart introduces fifteen verses, specifically for young children, along with devotions to help them know how the verse applies to them. These short passages are perfect for morning devotions or for bedtime prayers!

More Words for a Young Heart
ISBN: 9798765504987

More Words for a Young Heart, the second book in the series, introduces fifteen new verses chosen especially for children. The short devotions tell children how the verse applies to them and are perfect for instilling the habit of devotion and prayer in the morning or at bedtime!

About Kharis Publishing:

Kharis Publishing, an imprint of Kharis Media LLC, is a leading Christian and inspirational book publisher based in Aurora, Chicago metropolitan area, Illinois. Kharis' dual mission is to give voice to under-represented writers (including women and first-time authors) and equip orphans in developing countries with literacy tools. That is why, for each book sold, the publisher channels some of the proceeds into providing books and computers for orphanages in developing countries so that these kids may learn to read, dream, and grow. For a limited time, Kharis Publishing is accepting unsolicited queries for nonfiction (Christian, self-help, memoirs, business, health and wellness) from qualified leaders, professionals, pastors, and ministers. Learn more at: https://kharispublishing.com/

CPSIA information can be obtained
at www.ICGtesting.com
Printed in the USA
JSHW052131250623
43581JS00006B/21